Cambridge Latin Course
Units IIIA and IIIB
Teacher's Handbo

Cambridge Latin Course

Units IIIA and IIIB

Teacher's Handbook

Second edition

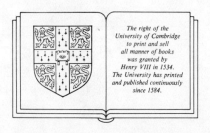

The right of the
University of Cambridge
to print and sell
all manner of books
was granted by
Henry VIII in 1534.
The University has printed
and published continuously
since 1584.

CAMBRIDGE UNIVERSITY PRESS

Cambridge

London   New York   New Rochelle

Melbourne   Sydney

Published by the Press Syndicate of the University of Cambridge
The Pitt Building, Trumpington Street, Cambridge CB2 1RP
32 East 57th Street, New York, NY 10022, USA
10 Stamford Road, Oakleigh, Melbourne 3166, Australia

This book, an outcome of work jointly commissioned by the Schools Council
before its closure and the Cambridge School Classics Project, is published under
the aegis of the School Curriculum Development Committee, Newcombe House,
45 Notting Hill Gate, London W11 3JB.

First published 1973
Reprinted 1978
Second edition 1985
Reprinted 1985

Printed in Great Britain at the University Press, Cambridge

ISBN 0 521 28752 9

Contents

Preface

For help in the preparation of Units IIIA and IIIB in their revised form, we should like to record our continued indebtedness to members of the Project team, editorial staff of the Cambridge University Press, the Project's Advisory Panel and others who were named and thanked in the Prefaces to the previous Handbooks. In addition, we should like to thank, for assistance of various kinds, Stephen Bird, John Briscoe, Barry Cunliffe, John Dawson, Roy Macdonald, Michael Massey, Paul Millett and Keith Sidwell.

D. J. Morton — Director
E. P. Story — Deputy Director
R. M. Griffin — Revision Editor
Cambridge School Classics Project

Cambridge 1985

Unit IIIA

Introduction

The Roman Britain episode, which began in Unit IIA and was interrupted by Quintus' narrative of events at Alexandria (Unit IIB), is concluded in Unit IIIA. Two themes are developed: a 'high life' story of political intrigue involving Salvius, Cogidubnus and the provincial governor, Agricola, and a 'low life' story in the manner of Roman comedy centred on two soldiers of the Second Legion, Modestus and Strythio. The early stages of the Unit are set in Roman Bath (Aquae Sulis) and illustrate features of Roman religious life. In the later stages the narrative moves to Chester (Deva) where the Second Legion was stationed at the time of these events, A.D.83. The theme of the Roman army is introduced.

The chief linguistic developments in this Unit involve:
1 perfect participles, first the perfect passive, then the perfect active (deponent) in Stages 21–3;
2 a range of clauses involving the use of imperfect and pluperfect subjunctive verbs: *cum* ('when'), indirect question, purpose, result and indirect command in Stages 24–7;
3 the ablative case. Pupils have been familiar with the ablative in prepositional phrases since Unit I, but in Stage 28 they meet it in other situations.

The Unit also revises the morphology of the verb in Stages 21–3, in readiness for the introduction of the subjunctive; and the noun in Stages 24–7, in readiness for the extension of the uses of the ablative. Revision exercises are included in the pupil's text and further suggestions for oral work will be found in the stage commentaries below.

The principles of teaching method discussed in the Unit I Teacher's Handbook pp. 15–27 continue to apply, including the need for variety within a lesson; for reading aloud; for giving pupils time to explore a portion of text by themselves; the use of comprehension questions both as an initial approach to the text and as a means of assessing pupils' understanding; and regular discussion of the subject matter of the stories.

Nevertheless, by this point the teacher may wish to modify previous routines to take account of the increased skill and maturity of the class and there should be a special concern to avoid monotony and maintain pace. The advice in the Unit I Handbook, p. 20, that it is not necessary to translate every word of each story, since this is a reading and not a translation course, applies particularly to the present Unit. The following means to variety may prove helpful:

1 the class may begin to study a passage by working in pairs or small groups, exploring the first two or three paragraphs to answer questions put by the teacher (for an example see p. 25 below, 'in thermīs') or in the pupil's text (see p. 64 below, 'in aulā Salviī');
2 after a story has been read the class can be asked to prepare and perform a dramatised reading instead of making a final translation (see p. 11 below, 'Memor rem suscipit');
3 regular short sessions of language consolidation can fit conveniently into the opening or ending of a lesson or make a useful transition activity in the middle of a double lesson.

It is hoped that variety will also be found in the content. New types of manipulation exercises have been introduced. The stories, although longer, on average, than in the previous Units, have been subdivided in some cases to take advantage of natural breaks.

Comprehension questions have been attached to some stories and they range from the straightforwardly factual ('What is the time of day at the start of this story?') to, increasingly, the interpretation of character and situation ('What do you think makes Cephalus smile and why does he try to hide the smile?'). Such questions, of course, can and should be asked on many occasions. Those printed are examples of what teachers will wish to devise themselves and use regularly, and to encourage this practice further we have added examples in the stage commentaries below. Comprehension questions are crucial for developing sensitive attention to what is being read and thereby laying good foundations for the critical enjoyment of literature.

The illustrations in the pupil's text also give opportunities for useful questions, sometimes on historical points ('What is the object on the left? What would be its purpose?'), sometimes in connection with the text ('Which sentence is illustrated by the picture?').

Another feature of teaching method deserves consideration: pupils should be given opportunities to work unaided. This is essential for building up fluency and confidence. But care should be taken not to push the class into working unaided on, say, a written translation of a long passage containing much unfamiliar language. The need to give pupils practice in working on their own needs to be weighed against the need to maintain success and a good pace.

There are numerous ways of keeping the balance. It may be done by working half an exercise orally in class and then asking pupils to write out the whole of it on their own. Another device is to guide the class in their first look at a passage, e.g. the teacher reads a portion aloud and conducts a brisk oral check of some key words in each sentence, before setting pupils to explore it on their own. Similarly, if the passage is suitable, the teacher may read it aloud twice and then ask the class to write down answers to straightforward comprehension questions. See suggestions on p. 25 below. It can also be beneficial gradually to increase the length of the portions which pupils are asked to look over by themselves. Again, the length of a portion that an individual is asked to translate aloud, after the first reading, should gradually be extended.

Related to this is the challenge to work without looking up vocabulary. Reliance on memory and context is obviously desirable when pupils are doing tests; it should also be encouraged as far as possible at other times.

Another means to variety is to duplicate exercises (either composed by the teacher or taken from the pupil's text) and ask pupils to write in the answer or tick the correct item. Alternatively, the overhead projector may be used for this purpose.

For teachers with a short time allowance the following passages and exercises are suggested for omission or, better, for accelerated reading. Omission of a story may leave a gap in the narrative or reduce the opportunity to practise a language feature. Therefore it is suggested that the teacher should normally translate these passages and work on selected sentences within them (see p. 27 below for an example of this approach).

Stage 21 'Lūcius Marcius Memor' I, lines 12–32 *or* II; exercise 4
Stage 22 'Modestus'
Stage 23 'epistula Cephalī'; exercise 3
Stage 24   exercise 2, exercise 4
Stage 25 'Modestus custōs'; exercise 2, exercise 3
Stage 26 'contentiō'; exercise 4
Stage 27 'sub horreō'; exercise 3.
Stage 28 'in aulā Salviī' II

It is, of course, also possible to save time by taking some exercises orally rather than having them written, provided that the teacher is satisfied that the needs of individual pupils are not being overlooked. Exercises of the completion type are especially suitable for this treatment.

Finally, the language notes in the pupil's text are, in many cases, printed late in the stages so that experience of the language feature will precede analysis. They may be taken earlier, if pupils seem ready, but never as an introduction to the stage. Whenever a note is taken, we advise strongly against asking pupils to read it through by themselves. Language notes necessarily make abstract statements; inevitably some pupils will experience difficulty in grasping them. The teacher should take the class through the note, which usually also contains a few practice examples. This will enable the teacher to adapt the note to the needs of the class, answer individual queries, and add other examples.

Filmstrip and cassette

Cambridge Classical Filmstrip 2, 'Roman Britain', contains visual
material suitable for use with Units IIA and IIIA. It includes the
following topics (asterisks indicate frames of particular relevance to Unit
IIIA):

Title frame–1	The conquest
2–14	Romanisation
15–22	Daily life
*23–29	Religion
*30–35	The army

In this Handbook, reference to particular frames is given by filmstrip
frame number, and also (where appropriate) by slide number for the
benefit of those teachers who are using the slides which accompanied the
first edition of the course. Unless otherwise stated, references are to
Filmstrip 2 and Unit III slides.

A further filmstrip (Cambridge Classical Filmstrip 4) contains new
material, i.e. material not taken from the original slides. It includes
several frames of special relevance to Unit IIIA.

The second cassette accompanying the course includes the following
material from Unit IIIA:

Stage 21	'Memor rem suscipit'
Stage 22	'amor omnia vincit' (three scenes)
Stage 23	'in thermīs' I and II
Stage 25	'Modestus̄ perfuga'
Stage 26	'contentiō'
Stage 28	'Belimicus rēx'

Stage commentaries

Books are normally referred to by the name of their author. For details of title, publisher, etc., see Bibliography, pp. 91–4.

A list of the linguistic features introduced and discussed in each stage is given in the 'Linguistic synopsis of Unit IIIA' on pp. 76–8.

STAGE 21: AQUAE SŪLIS

Synopsis

Reading passages	{ Roman Bath { Memor the soothsayer (continued in Stage 23)
Background material	Roman Bath
Language notes	perfect passive participle partitive genitive

Title picture

This shows the interior of the Great Bath, as it was at the end of the first century A.D. It will be useful for establishing the change of scene from Alexandria in Unit IIB. For a description of the Great Bath, see p. 13 below. Note the conduit bringing the water from the sacred spring in the far corner and the fountain half-way down the right-hand side. The doorway just visible through the pillars at the far end leads to the hall where the Stage 22 model sentences are set. Pupils may also like to see filmstrip 23 (slide 1).

Model sentences

These deal with the building of the baths. Some of the sentences contain new vocabulary but the pictures supply strong clues to the meaning. Some discussion of the cultural details in the pictures will be useful.

Three men are at work. The first, a sculptor, is making the head for a statue of Sulis Minerva. The second workman is putting the coping-stones on the wall that the Romans built around the spring itself. The third workman is bringing water in buckets, perhaps to make mortar or wash down newly laid paving-slabs. The main water supply from the spring to the Great Bath was through the pipe shown in the pictures (see also slides 2 and 3). The architect's final jibe, '*linguam sordidam habēs. melius est tibi aquam sacram bibere*', hints at the curative properties of the water.

The model sentences introduce the perfect passive participle. Occasional examples have already occurred but were treated as adjectives. Now the verbal aspect becomes prominent and the examples more numerous. Here and in the following two stories, the participle is limited to the forms ending in *-ātus* (*laudātus*) and *-ītus* (*arcessītus*). In the model sentences themselves, each participle is preceded by an example of the finite form of the verb; thus *laudātus* is anticipated by *laudāvit* etc. The first three participles are masculine singular nominative; one plural example is introduced near the end. A further support is provided by expressing the agent, e.g. *ab architectō laudātus*, thereby emphasising the participle's passive force.

Pupils will probably feel more secure at first if encouraged to use a standard form of translation for this participle, for instance *laudātus* = 'having been praised' or, perhaps less awkward, 'after being praised'. But as soon as they are able to recognise the participle readily they should be encouraged to use normal English equivalents, e.g. 'after he had been praised'; for flexibility in handling the participle is one of the most important skills the learner needs to acquire.

Perhaps the first natural variation is to omit the 'having been' and to say simply 'praised'. Examples where this rendering is appropriate will be found early in the stage: for instance, in 'fōns sacer', *prope thermās stat templum . . . ā meīs fabrīs aedificātum* (lines 13–14), where the version 'a temple built by my workmen' is more idiomatic English than 'a temple having been built . . .'.

Again, a pupil may translate *faber, ab architectō laudātus, laetissimus erat* by 'The workman was praised by the architect and was very pleased.' It would be misguided to reject this as wrong. A suitable response would be to say, 'Good. That gives the sense of the Latin, but can you put it a little differently and do without the "and"?' Pupils in their early teens are usually just acquiring the participle in English and hence often have a preference for the finite verb.

One other new language feature appears in the model sentences (one example only): the neuter plural, *īnsolentia verba*. The context, however, is clear and no comment will be required at this point. A language note in Stage 23 will discuss neuter plurals.

The following words are new: *oppidō, fabrī* (new meaning), *exstruēbant, sculpēbat, minimē* (new meaning), *īnsolenter, verba, linguam*.

fōns sacer

The scene shifts back to Fishbourne where Cogidubnus, now seriously ill,
contemplates a visit to Bath where he hopes to be cured by the waters.
The guardian deity of the spring was the Celtic goddess Sul or Sulis. (The
latter form of her name is used here.) In the stories we have imagined that
Cogidubnus himself played a part in the development of the temple and
baths. This is possible since the spring lay in territory which he may have
controlled; the buildings date from the late first century A.D. Now that
the model sentences and the first story have introduced the topic of the
baths, it will be a convenient moment for teachers to discuss the
background material.

Cogidubnus' attitude, expressed in the words *'ego deam saepe honōrāvī;
nunc fortasse dea mē sānāre potest'* (lines 14–15) may strike pupils as naïve or
irreligious by its implication of a bargain between worshipper and deity,
but it is an authentic Roman attitude towards the gods. Motives for
worship included the hope of favours in return, especially favours
concerned with health and safety. Teachers may wish to touch briefly on
religious attitudes here; a fuller treatment will be found in Stage 23.

The passive participle continues for the moment to be supported by *ā*
or *ab* with the agent (with one exception: *ad aulam arcessītī*, line 5). The
support is reduced in subsequent stories by replacing the agent with an
adverb or other prepositional phrase; finally the participle appears on its
own. If pupils translate *ā rēge invītātus* (line 2) as 'by the king's invitation',
the teacher should accept this as conveying the sense but ask for a more
literal rephrasing to check that the phrase has been perceived clearly.

Two other linguistic developments should be noted:
volō tē mihi cōnsilium dare (lines 8–9) and similar sentences. They closely
resemble their English equivalent in structure and are unlikely to cause
difficulty;
vir magnae prūdentiae (line 8). Pupils may find it helpful to treat these
descriptive genitive phrases literally at first, but variety should be
encouraged as soon as possible. A language note appears in Stage 22.

Lūcius Marcius Memor

Memor is a historical figure though later than our period (his character as
depicted in the stages is entirely fictitious); his name and presence at Bath
are attested by a statue base still standing in the temple precinct (see page
11, and filmstrip 25; slide 5), discovered in 1965. The inscription is shown
opposite. On this evidence Memor was a member of the priestly college of
haruspices and therefore involved in the administration of the baths and
temple. The narrative imagines him in charge of the religious community

DEAE SVLI
L MARCIVS MEMOR
HARVSP
D   D

(HARVSP = *haruspex;* DD = *dōnō dedit*)

and a leading figure in the government of the town. Although less
important than Salvius he belongs to the equestrian order and is a man of
some substance. It is interesting that the temple of Bath was sufficiently
important to attract a man of this status.

However, in the hierarchy of Roman priests a haruspex ranked lower
than a pontifex or an augur and Memor's hopes of *maiōrēs honōrēs* (I, line
28) demonstrate his present position within the system. No doubt he also
regarded a move to Rome as likely to benefit his career prospects; the
province of Britain must have been outside the consciousness of most
Romans most of the time. More details about haruspices will be found in
Stage 23, pp. 53–4 and pp. 30–1 below.

The policy of romanisation which Cephalus ironically attributes to
Memor was practised systematically by Agricola according to Tacitus,
Agricola 21. Memor was part of the process of bringing the two cultures
together and of superimposing, to some extent, the Roman upon the
Celtic. So the deity Sulis became Sulis Minerva; tribal leaders began to
live in Roman-style villas, do business in newly built forums and basilicas,
wear the toga and mix socially with the conquerors. The extent of the
change is debatable. Much may have been superficial. Maybe twenty or
thirty miles away from the romanised towns little change took place in the
Celtic patterns of life.

This story is divided into two parts. The questions following Part I are
meant to be studied by pupils, preferably in pairs or small groups, after a
first fairly rapid reading. Most of the questions are concerned with
character and motive, but question 3 can prompt a discussion of the
activities around the baths. After Part II the following questions could
also be discussed; they too require interpretive responses rather than
straightforward comprehension:

What does Memor find tiresome about his work at Bath?
Where would he prefer to be? Why?
What impression do you gain of the way he is doing his job?
When Cephalus announces the arrival of Salvius, what effect does the
    news have upon Memor?

For language work, continue practising the verb. This may be done on
a question-per-line basis, for example:

in line 1 'What tense is *erat*? Translate it.'
in line 2 'Find a verb in the imperfect tense. Translate it.'

Note that requests to identify words by their grammatical descriptions should normally be accompanied by a request to translate, so that description and translation remain closely associated in pupils' minds.

First language note (perfect passive participle)

After taking the class through the note on pp. 12–13 ask pupils to pick out examples of perfect participles in 'Lūcius Marcius Memor' and to say which noun each describes. The main need at this point is to develop the ability to
1 identify perfect participles in the text (teachers should accept the adjectival *perterritus, vexātus*);
2 translate them appropriately;
3 distinguish between the perfect participle and the present participle (several examples of which also occur in 'Lūcius Marcius Memor');
4 link the participle to its associated noun.
These skills are more important than mastery of the term 'passive', which has been postponed to the end of the language note and is included there only to pave the way for the term 'active' in Stage 22.

Paragraph 5 concentrates on agreement of number. When pupils have become more familiar with participles it will be helpful to return to this note and consider also agreement of gender. Examples here include the feminine *laudāta* (para. 4) and *parāta* (para. 6) and one neuter, *ōrnātum* (para. 2). Other neuter examples can be drawn from the stories.

Memor rem suscipit

This passage gives scope for pupils to explore the feelings, attitudes, and intentions of the characters. The dialogue portrays a battle of wills, which should be explored first by questions and then perhaps with a dramatic reading. Possible questions include:

Why does Salvius call Memor *vir summae prūdentiae* (line 2)?
Are Memor's first words true? What dilemma is he caught in?
What does Memor think Salvius is asking of him, when the latter says *Cogidubnus, quī in morbum gravem incidit, aquam ē fonte sacrō bibere vult* (lines 8–9)?
What arguments does Salvius employ to overcome Memor's scruples (or fear)?
Do you expect Memor to execute the plan? Why?
Why do you suppose Memor passes the task on to Cephalus?

Why is it difficult for Cephalus to refuse?

Why does Salvius proceed deviously instead of killing Cogidubnus
   directly with sword or dagger?

Pupils usually enjoy speculating about the technical details of the goblet
used for the poison. Their attention might be drawn to other mechanical
contrivances such as the eagle escaping from the wax effigy in Stage 15 or
Nero's booby-trapped ship intended to kill his mother Agrippina
(Tacitus, *Annals* XIV.3–6).

Finally, have the passage read aloud by some of the better readers in
the class. (In order to involve more pupils the parts of Memor and Salvius
might be divided between two readers each.) Before the reading is
performed it will be helpful to discuss key moments in the dialogue and
consider how they should be read. Part of the value of helping pupils to
read aloud intelligently is that it obliges them to study the text closely and
think about questions of character, mood and motive. For example,
Memor, in his first speech, replies hastily to Salvius' unspecified request
but pauses before *sed quid vīs mē facere?* as the possible seriousness of it
begins to dawn. His *quid dīcis?* in line 15 registers incredulity. In lines 21–6
Salvius tries to coax his man, finishing on a note that could be either
wheedling or menacing, *num praemium recūsāre vīs, tibi ab Imperātōre
prōmissum?*

After Salvius' departure Memor's next two speeches are extremely
anxious in tone, but in his last two speeches his mood changes rapidly,
perhaps because he begins to believe the feasibility of Cephalus'
suggestion but even more because he sees an opportunity to pass the buck.
Hence his final sardonic comment, *vīta, mī Cephale, est plēna rērum difficilium*,
mirrors exactly the tone of Salvius' utterance of these words in line 31.
The passage is also on the cassette.

Language practice after reading the story could consist of:
1 picking out the perfect participles and the nouns they describe (seven
   examples);
2 consolidating the use of the dative case with verbs such as *cōnfidere*. Put
   up on the blackboard the sentence *nūllīs tamen servīs cōnfidere ausim* (lines
   48–9), retranslate and then take the class through further examples
   such as *Memor Cephalō cōnfidit. Cephalus rēgī pōculum offert.*

Second language note (partitive genitive)

It may be useful to invite comparison with the similar French usage, e.g.
plus de vin, assez d'argent. Pupils could be asked to suggest why the genitive
case is used in Latin in such phrases as *plūs cibī, nimium vīnī*: each indicates
a quantity or part *of* something. More important, however, is to compare

the Latin with the natural English equivalents 'more food', 'too much wine'.

Further oral work could be done with harder phrases in which the genitive depends on *nihil* or *aliquid*, e.g. *nihil perīculī, aliquid novī. aliquid* may be linked to a genitive adjective, as above, which has to be translated by 'something new' or 'some news', or it may be linked to a genitive noun, e.g. *aliquid vīnī*, translated by 'some wine'.

Manipulation exercises

(In this and other stages that contain numerous exercises, it would be undesirable to work through all of them consecutively. Variety may be obtained by, for instance, doing Exercise 1 before some of the stories have been read.)

Exercise 1   Type: vocabulary
              Linguistic feature being practised: adverbs ending in -*ē*
This is the first of a series of exercises designed to increase pupils' ability to handle vocabulary by looking at cognate forms. They are intended for oral work. (If occasionally written, they should be done without 'looking-up'; otherwise the exercise becomes pointless.) The words include some that pupils have encountered before and others that are new, to make the point that words not previously met can be interpreted correctly if a cognate form is known. Encourage pupils to attempt their own generalisation about the way that adverbs are formed from adjectives ending in -*us*. The exercise could be extended with similar examples. Alternatively put a selection of the adverbs into short sentences and have them translated.

Exercise 2   Type: completion
              Missing item: noun
              Criterion of choice: morphology
              Linguistic feature being practised: nominative, accusative
                 and genitive cases, singular and plural

Exercise 3   Type: completion
              Missing item: noun *or* verb
              Criterion of choice: sense and syntax
              Linguistic feature being practised: sentence structure
If this exercise is thought difficult for pupils, it may be helpful to have the items in the pool translated orally before pupils do the exercise by themselves in writing.

Exercise 4   Type: translation from English, using restricted pool of Latin
                 words

Linguistic features being practised: nominative, accusative,
genitive and dative, singular and plural; perfect tense
In setting this exercise teachers should first do one or two sentences orally,
encouraging pupils to explain the reason for their choice and writing the
correct version on the blackboard. Ensure that pupils understand what is
required and know how to use the Language Information pamphlet to
help themselves. For the purpose of the exercise the position of the dative
is later than it normally is in the stories.

Exercise 5   Type: completion
Missing item: verb
Criterion of choice: morphology
Linguistic features being practised: 1st, 2nd and 3rd persons
singular of present, imperfect, perfect and pluperfect
(including one example of imperfect of *possum*)
This exercise may be useful to ascertain whether any particular inflexion
has not yet been grasped consistently.

The background material

The outstanding feature of the Roman town of Aquae Sulis was the group
of buildings consisting of the temple of Sulis Minerva, the temple precinct
and the suite of baths. The plan on p. 20 shows the complex at its earliest
stage. The visitor entered through the doorway at the bottom left and
passed through the frigidarium to reach the hall overlooking the sacred
spring, in which the Stage 22 model sentences are set. The doorway to the
Great Bath was then on his right (see title picture and photograph on
p. 21). This bath, lined with lead sheets, was 22 m long, 9 m wide and
1.5 m deep (72 × 29 × 5 ft) and was entered by steps along all four sides.
Warm water flowed into it through a lead pipe that ran directly from the
sacred spring. Round the bath ran wide ambulatories paved with hard
limestone. On each of the long sides were three recesses (*exedrae*), which
provided sitting areas well clear of splashing water. The roof was probably
about 13.5 m (44 ft) above the bath and the upper walls must have
contained apertures to allow daylight to enter and steam to escape.

The photograph on p. 21 shows the Great Bath as it is today, looking in
the opposite direction to the title picture. The columns and superstructure
are Victorian. The Roman lead lining survives but originally covered the
steps as well. The block of masonry in the bath is part of the early third-
century stone vault which replaced the wooden roof of the first century.
The hollow box tiles from which it was constructed to save weight can be
seen.

The spring which supplied the baths with their constant hot water was
enclosed within the south-east corner of the temple precinct. The Romans

lined the spring with lead sheets and built a wall round it (see 'Model sentences', pp. 6–7 above). Many items were thrown into it as offerings to the goddess, like the pewter and silver bowls in the photograph on p. 22. These may have been part of the temple plate; they were used for pouring libations and are inscribed with dedications to the goddess. They show signs of wear and may have been consigned to the goddess' spring when worn out. In the centre of the precinct stood the temple. Much of it lies beneath the present abbey but modern techniques have made excavation possible and allowed archaeologists to examine the site. It cannot be definitely dated but was probably first built in the first century A.D. with modifications later. Work is still proceeding on reconstructing it. For detailed accounts see Cunliffe *Roman Bath Discovered* or his more elaborate *Roman Bath*.

One of the most interesting discoveries is the pediment of the temple (see drawing on p. 45) which has been pieced together from fragments. In the centre is a Gorgon's head (see filmstrip 24; slide 4), with snaky hair and, unusually, a male face with moustaches in the Celtic style. Supporting it on either side are winged Victories carved in the classical manner. This blend of styles denotes more than a meeting of different artistic traditions; it is a powerful example of religious syncretism. The local Celtic deity Sulis has become identified with the Roman Minerva, represented by the Gorgon's head which she traditionally carried upon her shield.

The town was smaller than a typical Roman market town. Although excavations have revealed a number of large private houses as well as taverns, lodging-houses and the homes of ordinary people, the site as a whole was not densely built up during the first century A.D. But its mineral baths ensured that Aquae Sulis was widely known and much visited. Regular repairs and modifications to the Great Bath and evidence of wear on steps and paving-stones testify to the constant passage of visitors. So too do the surviving inscriptions which are mainly of two kinds: tombstones, and altars erected in thanksgiving for a safe journey or in hope of a cure. In addition to Memor, the name of one priest is known, Gaius Calpurnius Receptus (see slide 7).

Tourism may have been the foundation of the town's economy, but the surrounding countryside was a prosperous agricultural, and to some extent industrial, area in which many large villas were established, sheep and cattle grazed and corn was grown. Stone was quarried and pewter, which was used as a cheap alternative to silver, was manufactured nearby from Cornish tin and the lead of the Mendip Hills.

Suggestions for discussion

1 Compare the interior of the Great Bath at Aquae Sulis with the baths

at Herculaneum (see, for example, Cambridge Classical Filmstrip 4). What similarities and differences may be observed? Which baths most resemble a modern swimming pool? Why?

2 Discuss the idea that a spring was a religious place. What objects would impress upon a visitor that he was in a religious setting when he came to the baths at Aquae Sulis?

3 Read in translation Tacitus, *Agricola* 21, and, using the example of Sulis Minerva and the religious complex at Bath, discuss the idea of romanisation.

Words and phrases checklist

Perfect participles are now included in the checklists with appropriate verbs. This may be useful for additional practice in translating participles. Discourage the notion that only the words in the checklists matter. Clearly the more vocabulary pupils know the better.

Suggestions for further work

1 Tell the story of the gradual discovery of Roman Bath. An excellent account, including excerpts from the Anglo-Saxon poem 'The Ruin' which almost certainly describes the site as it appeared in the eighth century, will be found in Cunliffe's *Roman Bath Discovered*. The latest information about the recent excavations is available from Bath City Council (address on p. 92 below).

2 With data from Cunliffe and other sources explore our knowledge of the people who lived in or visited Bath. Invite pupils to write an imaginary biography of someone appearing in an inscription, using such factual details as are available.

3 Show pupils filmstrip 27, the model of the Temple of Claudius at Colchester, or another picture of a temple. Discuss the similarities with and differences from the temple at Bath.

STAGE 22: DĒFĪXIŌ

Synopsis

Reading passages }
Background material } magic and superstition

Language notes   perfect active participle
                    descriptive genitive

Title picture

For this *dēfīxiō* see pages 19 and 21–2 below.

Model sentences

An offering to the goddess is retrieved by a thief from the sacred spring. It bears an appropriate curse. The idea of invoking divine help against actual or potential enemies will reappear in the stories and the background material of this stage. The episode takes place in the hall outside the Great Bath with the windows, one round-headed flanked by two square, looking over the sacred spring. Two of these windows can still be seen (see photograph on p. 35).

All the perfect participles in Stage 21 were passive. Now the perfect active participle is introduced. The term 'perfect active' is employed instead of 'perfect deponent' in order not to muddle pupils' perception of the contrast between the active and passive voices that needs to be the focal point of attention. Deponent verbs, together with the term 'deponent', are introduced in Stage 32, and use of the term should be postponed until then.

The pictures and story line, supported by the teacher's comprehension questions, offer such powerful clues to the meaning that pupils normally have little difficulty in handling the new feature. Let discussion of the difference between the perfect active participles of this stage and the perfect passive participles in Stage 21 follow the reading not only of the model sentences but of one or more stories in the stage. Such discussion will be more effective when pupils have successfully encountered several examples in context. If, for example, a pupil renders *fūr thermās ingressus* as 'the thief having been entered ... ', the remedy is to put the concrete question 'Who entered the baths?'

Pupils may also tend to translate perfect participles as present ones, because English readily uses the present participle for the perfect, as for instance in the sentence 'Entering the baths the thief ... '. However, while pupils are learning the important distinctions of voice and tense in the participle it is desirable to keep clear what the tense of the participle is. Again, the teacher should prefer concrete to abstract guidance. So, with this example, instead of labouring the terms 'present' and 'perfect', it would be better to ask 'Did the thief enter the baths and look round at the same time? If he entered *before* he looked round, how could we put that clearly in English?' This opens the way for a range of alternative renderings, e.g. 'When he had entered ... ', 'Having entered ... ' or 'After entering ... '.

The following words are new: *ingressus, cōnspicātus, columnam, precātus, regressus, adeptus.*

Vilbia

The stories of this stage look at the life of ordinary people in Bath. The presentation is not too serious. Vilbia and Rubria are the daughters of the innkeeper Latro. Vilbia has fallen for the smooth tongue of Modestus, a Roman soldier on leave from Chester. Teachers will recognise as his original, the braggart warrior Pyrgopolynices in Plautus' *Miles Gloriosus*, while his friend, Strythio, is modelled on the parasite, Artotrogus, in the same play. Bulbus is a local boy jilted by Vilbia in favour of the glamorous soldier.

Dialogue dominates throughout. It serves not only to reveal character and define relationships but also as the principal vehicle for the humour; thus each speaker builds on, caps or rebukes what the other has just said, scoring points in the process. Help pupils to catch the tone by asking, for instance, whether Rubria really sympathises with her sister's feelings or is out to make mischief. Perhaps the main question to explore is, 'Why has Vilbia abandoned Bulbus for Modestus?' Pupils will recognise that it is Modestus' braggadocio manner that has won her heart. She has also fallen for Modestus' physical attractions (*quantī erant lacertī eius*) and apparent integrity (*Modestus probus*). Pupils may surmise that her judgement has been influenced by the gift of a handsome brooch.

Let the discussion remain within the terms of comedy; for questions about the relationship of Roman soldiers with British women probably require more than average maturity on the part of the class. No doubt in the early days of Roman occupation reactions were mixed; some women would deliberately avoid contact, while others would willingly or unwillingly have become prostitutes. The growth of civilian *vīcī* outside forts, on the other hand, testifies to the development of lasting relationships, even though for the soldier the relationship could not be acknowledged as a legal marriage until after his discharge.

Examples of descriptive genitive phrases begin from line 3, *vir magnae dīligentiae sed minimae prūdentiae.* No comment is required until the language note on p. 37, but some variety of translation ought to be encouraged, e.g. 'a man of great diligence', 'a hard-working man', 'a man who worked hard'.

The position of *autem* (line 20) may call for attention. Put the sentence on the board, ask for a translation, put that on the board and invite comment about the positions in the sentence of *autem* and 'but'. When the position of *autem* has been noted, ask pupils to recall other connecting words that are placed in this position (*enim, igitur* and *tamen*).

If pupils feel that 'heart-throb' (in the glossary) is too old-fashioned as a translation of *suspīrium*, invite alternative suggestions. The literal meaning, 'a sigh', might be mentioned.

Modestus

This short piece of dialogue introduces the principal male characters, Modestus and Strythio, both on leave from the Second Legion at Chester. Of the two Modestus is a straightforward windbag, though evidently possessed of some charm. Strythio is rather more complex, since he both depends on Modestus and makes a fool of him. Teachers might suggest to pupils at the beginning that they look out for differences between these two so that they can produce brief character sketches.

Ask pupils to keep an eye on links between this and the previous story. For instance, Strythio's remark *Vilbia . . . statim amāvit* (line 9) confirms Vilbia's claim that it was love at first sight. Strythio, lines 13–15, also confirms that Modestus had given her the brooch but adds more detail.

First language note (perfect active participle)

The note introduces the term 'perfect active participle', illustrates it with several examples and contrasts it with the perfect passive. The note accounts for the difference between them simply in terms of different translations, 'having . . .' and 'having been . . .'. The fact that these participles belong to different categories of verb is not discussed until Stage 32, but appears in the Language Information pamphlet, pp. 15 and 29.

If pupils ask 'How can I tell whether a perfect participle is active or passive?', show them how to use the context as a guide, saying, for example, 'Look at the whole sentence. It doesn't just say *parātus*, but *ā servīs parātus*. Which makes better sense, "having prepared by the slaves" or "having been prepared by the slaves"?' Or 'Look at the sentence *Modestus, thermās ingressus, avidē circumspectat*. Would it make sense to translate "Modestus having been entered"? Look at *thermās* next to *ingressus*. How will that fit in?' When the participle is treated in this way pupils are likely to take it in their stride. Some mistakes will of course be made, but they are resolved better by taking pupils back to familiar examples than by embarking on analysis in terms of passive/deponent.

amor omnia vincit

scaena prīma

In Latro's inn Bulbus is drinking and dicing with his friend Gutta, until

interrupted by the entry of Modestus and Strythio. As the pictures on
p. 32 show, Roman dice had six faces with the same markings as modern
dice. A 'Venus' was a double six, a 'dog' was a double one. Some pupils
may find Bulbus' run of bad luck suspicious; this would be a suitable
moment to mention the loaded dice discovered at Vindolanda, which
produces a six 8 times out of 10.

The *tabula* Bulbus talks about in lines 20–2 is the one illustrated on the
title-page and filmstrip 26 (slide 8), which was found in Bath. It is
discussed below on pp. 21–2.

Language work in this and the next scene could usefully concentrate on
the verb. There is plenty of scope for oral and written conversion
exercises. Begin, perhaps, with the teacher making the substitution while
inviting pupils to supply the meaning, for instance 'What did *āmīsistī* in
line 4 mean? What would *āmīsī* mean? What did *iactāvī* in line 8 mean?
What would *iactāvit* mean?' Then, abler pupils could be asked to change
āmīsistī, line 4, to the form meaning 'I lost', then 'he lost'. Keep the tense
unchanged at first. Then, more difficult, retain the person but change the
tense. Finally, see if pupils can change both tense and person in one step.

scaena secunda

Deserted by Gutta, Bulbus has to face alone the anger of the two soldiers,
but Vilbia's intervention saves him from further punishment. Modestus
presses Vilbia to meet him later. For a moment she hesitates, then accedes
to the pleas of her lover. Pupils might comment on her reasons for (1)
trying to save Bulbus from further maltreatment, (2) her abrupt change of
mind, line 19. Ask them to suggest the best way to convey this change
when reading aloud *pater mē sōlam exīre nōn vult. ubi est hic locus?*

For language work the opportunity should be taken again to check and
consolidate pupils' mastery of verb endings. For example, 'In line 6 what
is the meaning of *verberāvistī*? What would be the meaning of *verberāvimus*?
In line 17 what is the meaning of *ēlēgistī*? What would be the meaning of
ēlēgī?'

The sentence pattern containing *possum* or *volō* + infinitive, e.g. *tibi
resistere nōn possum* (lines 23–4), is well represented here. This too could be
practised by a substitution exercise. The teacher changes the person of the
finite verb, e.g. *possumus* for *potest*, or replaces the infinitive with that of
another suitable verb, writes the sentence on the board and asks pupils to
translate.

The photograph on p. 35 shows the sacred spring, looking back at the
windows featured in the model sentences. The surrounding buildings are
not ancient but the square window and the round-headed one to the right
of it are Roman with modern infilling.

scaena tertia

The villain gets his deserts.

The position of the dative case in the sentence is now more varied, in accordance with normal Latin usage.

There are opportunities in this passage for practising the use of *nōlī/ nōlīte* + infinitive. Examples can be picked out and contrasted with the corresponding positive command, for instance, *nōlī lacrimāre* (line 35) with *lacrimā, stā prope fontem* (line 10) with *nōlī stāre prope fontem*. Develop into the plural with *stāte* and *nōlīte stāre*.

Some suggested questions

How does Bulbus overcome Gutta's reluctance to put on a woman's dress?

Modestus describes himself, line 15, as *fortissimus mīlitum*. Does he behave like this when attacked by Bulbus? Why not?

Bulbus claims, line 28, that he could now easily kill Modestus, and the latter does not seem to doubt it. Why?

When Vilbia hears Modestus readily give her up, *nōn amō Vilbiam* (line 29), how does she react? What does Bulbus say to calm her fury?

These three scenes are suitable for acting by groups. Four speaking (and two non-speaking) parts are required. They also go well as a tape-recording, which has the advantage that it can be rehearsed and recorded in small sections and then be 'performed' by playing it back straight through. The sound effects include: the rattle of dice, grunts and groans of men fighting and if possible the splash when Modestus is pushed into the water. Another method is to have the play read aloud dramatically and with sound effects, but without acting. Older pupils may prefer this approach.

The play has been recorded on the cassette. It would be worthwhile, especially with able pupils, to let them listen to the recording (after having read the play) following it by ear alone.

Second language note (descriptive genitive)

Pupils will probably feel more secure if, to begin with, they are allowed to use the familiar 'of' translation. Encourage them, however, to be more adventurous as soon as they are used to these phrases.

Manipulation exercises

Exercise 1   Type: vocabulary
             Linguistic feature being practised: adverbs in *-ter*

Exercise 2   Type: completion
            Criterion of choice: morphology
            Linguistic feature being practised: dative and genitive,
               singular and plural

Exercise 3   Type: sentence composition from pool of Latin words
            Linguistic features being practised: nominative, accusative
               and dative, singular and plural; 3rd person singular and
               plural of perfect

Pupils might work in pairs, taking it in turns to devise a sentence for the
other to translate. Encourage natural Latin word order and the use of as
many different words as possible; but the main object is the correct choice
of inflexions from the word pool. Also encourage the production of
sentences whose meaning is plausible. Pupils may attempt to use words
not in the pool or words from the pool in different forms and this can cause
difficulty. Teachers can help by asking them to consult about their ideas
before producing the finished version.

The background material

Dēfixiōnēs or formal curses that consecrate one's enemy to the gods of the
Underworld have been found in considerable numbers in Roman Britain.
The tablet on which the stories of this stage are based was found at Bath
and reads as follows:

> [I]VQ IHIM MAIBLIV TIVALO/[V]NI CIS TAVQIL
> (OD)[O]MOC AVQA / [A]LLE ATVM IVQ MAE TIVA/[RO]V
> IS ANNIVLEV SVEREPV/SXE SVNAIREV SVNIREV/ES
> SILATSVG(V)A SVNAITI/MOC SVNAINIMSVTAC /
> [A]LLINAMREG ANIVOI   (*R.I.B.*154)

The backward writing is quite a common feature of defixio tablets; when
the order of the letters is reversed this inscription emerges as:

> QVI MIHI VILBIAM INVOLAVIT SIC LIQVAT[1] COMO(DO)[2]
> AQVA ELLA[3] MVTA QVI EAM VORAVIT SI VELVINNA
> EXSVPEREVS VERIANVS SEVERINVS A(V)GVSTALIS
> COMITIANVS CATVSMINIANVS GERMANILLA IOVINA

([1] = *liquēscat* [or = *liqueat*], [2] = *quōmodō*, [3] = *illa*)

The text and its interpretation are uncertain in parts. A translation of the
version given above reads:

> May he who has stolen Vilbia from me dissolve like water. May she
> who has devoured her be struck dumb, whether it be Velvinna or
> Exsupereus or Verianus, *etc.*

The number of possible candidates to be cursed perhaps says more about Vilbia than about those who caused her lover's jealousy. Teachers might put up on the board the part of the curse printed at the beginning of the stage (i.e. as far as AVQA), rewrite the letters in the usual order with help from the class and work out a version.

A large collection of defixiones in the form of lead scrolls was discovered in 1980 at Uley, some miles north of Bath, on the site of a small temple of Mercury which probably also served as a meeting-place and market. It seems likely that the curses were drawn up by the temple clerk at the request of local people, mainly farmers, who were perhaps 'hedging their bets' in a legal case against a neighbour. If so, it was a fairly public way of cursing one's enemy and suggests the importance of ensuring that he got to know about it. Clearly such curses were more than a conventional ritual. Many, both Roman and Celt, must have believed that they could be an effective instrument of vengeance. Further discussion of superstition will be found in Paoli 279–91; Balsdon 65–7.

The defixio tablet on p. 41 of the pupil's text shows a demon in a boat. He may be a representation of Charon, the ferryman who carried the souls of the dead over the Styx. The figure holds an urn and a torch, symbols of death. The text on the left reads CVIGEV, CENSEV, CINBEV, PERFLEV, DIARVNCO, DIASTA, BESCV, BEREBESCV, ARVRARA, BAGAGRA: on the demon's breast, ARITMO, ARAITTO: on the boat, NOCTIVAGVS, TIBERIS, OCEANVS. See Paoli 285–6.

The reverse of the tablet reads: ADIVRO TE DEMON QVICVMQVE ES ET DEMANDO TIBI EX ANC DIE EX AC ORA EX OC MOMENTO VI EQVOS PRASINI ET ALBI CRVCIES ET AGITATORES CLARVM ET FELICEM ET PRIMVLVM ET ROMANVM OCIDAS COLLIDAS NEQVE SPIRITVM ILLIS LERINQVAS: ADIVRO TE PER EVM QVI TE RESOLVIT TEMPORIBVS DEVM PELAGI CVM AERIVM IAW LASDAW . . .

I adjure you, demon, whoever you are, and I demand of you, from this day from this hour from this moment, that you torture the horses of the Greens and the Whites and destroy and smash their drivers Clarus and Felix and Primulus and Romanus and leave no breath in them. I adjure you by that god of the sea who has released you in due season and by the god of the air, Iaw . . .

(Quoted in Dudley 215)

It has been suggested that the names on the boat are those of the horses being cursed. The tablet was written in the third century A.D. at Hadrumetum in North Africa and was found in a tomb.

Here are some other defixiones that have been discovered in Britain:

(a) TRETIA(M) MARIA(M) DEFICO ET / ILLEVS VITA(M) ET
ME(N)TEM / ET MEMORIAM [E]T IOCINE/RA PULMONES
INTERMIX/TA ... SCI[1] NO(N) POSSITT LOQVI / (QVAE)
SICRETA SI(N)T ...   (*R.I.B.*7)

(^{1} = *sīc*)

I curse Tretia Maria, her life, mind, memory, liver and lungs mixed
up together. Thus may she be unable to speak what is hidden ...

(b) DONATVR DEO IOVI / OPTIMO MAXIMO VT / EXIGAT
PER MENTEM PER / MEMORIAM PER INTVS / PER
INTESTINVM PER COR / [P]ER MEDVLLAS PER VENAS /
... SI MASCEL SI / FEMINA QVI(SQ)VIS / INVOLAVIT
DENARIOS CANI / DIGNI VT IN CORPORE / SVO IN BREVI
TEMP[OR]E / PARIAT DONATVR / DEO DECIMA PARS
(*Journal of Roman Studies*, vol. 53 (1963) pp. 122–4)

This tablet is given to Jupiter Optimus Maximus with the prayer that
he may smite through the mind, memory, inward parts, guts, heart,
marrow, veins whatever person, man or woman, has stolen the money
of Canus Dignus. Let him quickly restore the money in person. A
tenth of the money is offered to the god.

(c) Among the 40 or so defixiones found in the spring at Bath was an
engagingly all-purpose insurance policy directed against an unknown
enemy *utrum vir, utrum mulier, utrum puer, utrum puella, utrum servus, utrum
liber*. Moreover, to ensure that the magic had the best chance of
working, the whole was written backwards (see Hassall in *Omnibus* I
and VI for this and other defixiones).

(d) At Lydney in Gloucestershire, there was an important temple of
Nodens, a Celtic god of hunting, who was also worshipped for his
healing powers. Defixiones were found there too, including one by a
certain Sylvianus who had had a ring stolen from him. Sylvianus
promised to pay the god half its value if it were recovered, and cursed
the suspected thief in the following terms: 'Among those who are
called Senecianus do not allow health until he brings the ring to the
temple of Nodens.' His suspicions about the identity of the culprit
may have been confirmed by archaeologists who discovered at
Silchester a ring engraved with the words 'Senecianus, may you rest
in God'. The formula suggests he may have been a Christian, but the
ring also carried the name Venus, pagan goddess of love, presumably
put there by the first owner, conceivably Sylvianus (see Birley, *Life*
147 and Branigan 259).

Suggestions for discussion

1   Put up on the board one or both of the defixiones (a) and (b) above (these were not originally written backwards), work out the meaning with contributions from the class and invite pupils to suggest either the incident that may have given rise to the curse or the possible outcome of it. This might begin as a class discussion and then lead to individual written work.

2   'What does the use of defixiones suggest about the popular conception of the gods?' If the class is sufficiently mature discuss the related but not necessarily overlapping ideas of 'a god as a powerful being' and of 'a god as having a moral will'.

3   Explore possible reasons for the widespread belief in defixiones and similar magico-religious practices. Such reasons may include: lack of confidence in the public system of justice; lack of scientific understanding of the natural world which increases a tendency to believe in irrational forces.

Suggestions for further work

1   Invite pupils to design an imaginary defixio of their own, including in it a drawing and magic words like those given on p. 22.

2   Ask groups of pupils to collect and write out some of the rhymes and formulae which they themselves, when younger, used to avert danger or express dislike of somebody.

STAGE 23: HARUSPEX

Synopsis

Reading passages	Memor the soothsayer (continued from Stage 21)
Background material	divination and religion
Language note	neuter plural

No new language features appear in this stage and so there are no model sentences. The principal task for the stage is consolidation of the perfect participle. Pupils should concentrate on:

associating the participle with the correct noun;

translating the participle appropriately, using a variety of English
equivalents;
distinguishing perfect active from perfect passive participles and both
of these from present participles.
Assess pupils' grasp initially by the correctness of their translation.
Gradually, follow this with the request to say whether the participle is
perfect active or perfect passive.

Title picture

This shows Memor examining the entrails of a lamb on the altar in the
temple precinct at Bath. The altar platform, which has survived, is
4.3 × 5.5 m (14 × 18 ft) and three corners of the altar have also been
found. They are carved with gods and goddesses on adjacent sides. For a
full description see Cunliffe, *Roman Bath Discovered* 22–3. The figure of
Memor is based on one of the figures from a second-century relief of
haruspices now in the Louvre (see slide 54).

in thermīs

The plot against Cogidubnus is resumed. Begin by reading the first two
paragraphs aloud; then ask pupils to work in pairs or small groups to look
for answers to comprehension questions such as these (put them on the
board and let pupils refer to the plan in Stage 21, p. 20):

Where does this ceremony take place? Who are present?
What kind of ceremony is it?
What happens in the second paragraph?
What state of mind does Memor seem to be in?

Then bring the class together, check that the story line has been
understood and read quickly the dialogue that follows. Two topics could
then be pursued:

1 Divination. Refer pupils first to the background material pp. 53–4 for
information, then invite them to say why Cogidubnus sacrificed a lamb
to Sulis Minerva before taking his treatment: firstly to enquire whether
he would recover and secondly, by making a present of the lamb, to try
to secure a favourable outcome. What reply did Sulis Minerva appear
to be making? If Memor had announced what the priest had actually
found in the liver, how might Cogidubnus have acted? (The gender of
agna might be noted in passing: a female animal is sacrificed to a female
deity.)

2 Memor's behaviour. Why is he trembling and sweating? Why does he
show alarm at the priest's statement that the liver is *līvidum* (line 12)? 'A

guilty conscience' or 'he thought the goddess was trying to warn Cogidubnus' may be sufficient comment. But note also he begins to panic. Memor lacks the coolness of Salvius.

The picture on p. 45 shows the exterior of the temple. Note the pediment, described on p. 14 above.

Pace is essential for the first reading of Part II. Perhaps most effective would be to read the Latin aloud pausing only to ask a brief comprehension question after each sentence. Some teachers enhance the effect by breaking off at the words *rēx pōculum ad labra sustulit* (line 15), resuming in the next lesson, by which time most pupils have read the next three lines on their own.

Cogidubnus' remark, *aqua est amāra, sed remedium potentissimum* (lines 11–12), refers, of course, to the naturally pungent taste of water with a mineral content; on this occasion he does not actually taste it at all since Quintus intervenes.

Both parts are on the cassette.

Some suggested questions

Why did the slaves find it difficult to lower the king into the bath? What do you think were the commands (*mandāta*) given by Cogidubnus at this moment? Why were the chiefs scolding their *lībertī*?

Why, after the king had emerged from the bath, did he approach the *fōns sacer*?

Why are the words *anxius tremēbat* used of Cephalus in line 14?

What caused Quintus to suspect the goblet was poisoned? Was his guess about its origin correct (see Stage 21, p. 15, line 41)?

How did Dumnorix propose finding out whether the contents were drugged?

epistula Cephalī

During the reading of this 'letter' pupils often notice discrepancies between what Cephalus claims and what actually took place. Encourage this by recalling the relevant part of Stage 21, 'Memor rem suscipit'. Pupils should also be asked to suggest the purpose of the letter. Cephalus had in fact attempted to poison Cogidubnus. Therefore could the letter have been a warning in advance? Perhaps it was insurance in case the plan miscarried and Cephalus found himself taking responsibility. This is the familiar practice of seeking to shift responsibility to the person who gave the orders. Finally pupils may be invited to speculate about Cogidubnus' response. Will he be sceptical? Or will he guess that

Cephalus and Memor were jointly responsible? Leave the outcome to emerge during 'Britannia perdomita'.

Linguistically 'epistula Cephalī' is straightforward. It provides a good opportunity to revise the 1st and 2nd persons singular of the verb particularly in the perfect tense. For this an oral substitution exercise as described above, p. 19, may be useful. Alternatively, pupils may be asked to pick out, for instance, the verbs in the perfect tense in lines 6–9 and then to identify which is 1st person. Various phrases with *rem* also occur. Idiomatic English equivalents for this general-purpose noun should be discussed and their use encouraged.

The passage is on the list of those that may be omitted (p. 4) if time is very short. However, teachers who feel that there is some time available but only a little, could translate the story to the class and then devote five minutes to language practice on it, for instance, by getting pupils to pick out the participles or look for and translate 1st and 2nd persons of the verb.

Language note (neuter plural)

Neuter plural nouns have occurred quite frequently since Stage 21, but comment has been postponed until this point. Paragraph 2 of the note invites the generalisation that all neuter plural nouns end in *-a* in both the nominative and accusative cases. It is better if this is elicited from the class rather than just handed down by the teacher. The class can then be directed to the paradigm of the adjective in the Language Information pamphlet, p. 7, and again asked to comment on the neuter plural ending. The same observation should be elicited.

Britannia perdomita

In the hands of such operators as Salvius and Memor the old king is helpless. Until it is brutally pointed out he fails to grasp that he no longer enjoys any standing with the government in Rome. The years of loyalty count for nothing now.

Motive is the essence of these political stories, and should be explored as the reading proceeds. What reasons are suggested to explain why Salvius conspired to bring down Cogidubnus? Why might Cogidubnus be aggrieved at Salvius' remark *numquam contentus fuistī. nōs diū vexāvistī* (line 31)? In answer pupils may quote the king's hospitable treatment of Salvius and his honouring of the Emperor Claudius (Unit IIA, Stages 15 and 16). The teacher might add historical evidence: Cogidubnus' possible role in the invasion of A.D.43 is considered in the Units IIA and IIB Handbook, p. 26, and Tacitus describes him as being *ad nostram usque memoriam fidissimus* (*Agricola* 14). So far as his past record was concerned, he might reasonably expect *fidēs Rōmāna* to continue towards himself. If then the alleged *arrogantia* of Cogidubnus is not the real reason for Domitian's movement against him, what might it be? A possible answer will be suggested in Stage 26 (p. 104).

Linguistically the passage offers opportunities for consolidating the various persons of the perfect tense; examples could be picked out by pupils and translated.

The questions following the passage seek to establish the protagonists' relative positions of power and to show how their actions were the outcome of assumptions and calculations. Discussion might be prefaced by a reminder of the situation at the start of the story. What do pupils suppose will be the king's feelings towards Memor at this moment? And what may be the mood of Salvius after the failure of his plot?

In dealing with question 1 invite consideration of the way Cogidubnus has dressed for this visit, *togam praetextam ōrnāmentaque gerit* (lines 3–4). In question 4 ensure that pupils understand that Cogidubnus has brought soldiers to put Memor out of his job. Was this a miscalculation? Or was it his best chance of dealing with the threat to his life? Salvius' reactions to Cogidubnus' display of force should be carefully noted. Was he surprised? Memor reacts to the confrontation by protesting innocence, *tū mē dēmōvistī? innocēns sum* (line 27), and is about to continue when Salvius cuts him off. Pupils may speculate whether Memor was about to appeal to Salvius for support or to accuse him. In question 5 the answer is of course *Rōmānum*. Invite suggestions for a good way to translate *in eādem sententiā mānsit* (line 24) and *nimium audēs* (lines 29–30). The last question looks for some consideration of Cogidubnus' state of mind at the end. What does he regret? What else could he have done at the time of the invasion?

There is no historical evidence for the letter which Salvius claims to have received from Domitian instructing him to expropriate the estates of Cogidubnus (lines 33–5), but an instruction of that kind would be consistent with what we know of Salvius' mission to Britain as *iūridīcus* (see the Units IIA and IIB Handbook, pp. 9–10). Cogidubnus certainly seems to have disappeared at this time; whether from natural causes or foul play is not known.

Pupils will probably see the sense of *id quod* in *id quod dīcis, absurdum est* (line 15). Confirm that the single word 'what' is sufficient as a translation. A short note and further practice appears in the Language Information pamphlet for Unit IIIB.

The coin pictured on page 49 is a didrachma from Caesarea, about A.D.46. It shows the Emperor Claudius in a chariot, holding an eagle-topped sceptre. The use of *dē* in this context ('a triumph over the Britons') is new to pupils.

Manipulation exercises and further practice

Exercise 1   Type: vocabulary
            Linguistic feature being practised: nouns ending in *-or*
Perfect participles are given where the cognate noun may seem remote
from the infinitive, e.g. *pingere (pictus) – pictor*. Teachers may like to add the
participles for the other verbs and so demonstrate that for all verbs the
noun derives from the perfect participle, e.g. *amāre (amātus) – amātor*. The
exercise can be extended with examples from other verbs, e.g. *nārrāre
(nārrātus) – nārrātor; agere (āctus) – āctor*.

Exercise 2   Type: completion
            Missing item: verb
            Criterion of choice: morphology
            Linguistic feature being practised: 1st, 2nd and 3rd persons
                plural of present, imperfect, perfect and pluperfect
Like Stage 21 Exercise 5, this is designed to revise the basic morphology of
the verb before the introduction of the imperfect and pluperfect
subjunctive active.

Exercise 3   Type: transformation
            Linguistic feature being practised: infinitive with present
                tense of *volō, possum* and *dēbeō*, introduced in Stages 13 and
                16
In this exercise the examples have been selected to avoid the complication
of vowel changes such as *scrībunt → scrībere*. If pupils have difficulty, let
them look up the form of the infinitive in the 'Words and phrases' section
of the Language Information pamphlet. Teachers may extend this
exercise by changing the verbs in the left-hand column (avoiding vowel
changes), or by switching the auxiliary verbs around.

Exercise 4   Type: completion
            Missing item: participle
            Criterion of choice: sense and syntax
            Linguistic feature being practised: perfect participles passive
                and active, introduced in Stages 21 and 22
As in the stories, let pupils be guided principally by the context. The noun
governing the participle is in every instance nominative singular
masculine.
    If teachers feel that more practice of the verb morphology is needed
before the subjunctive is introduced, some of the following transformation
exercises may be helpful:

    1   'Suppose the first paragraph of "in thermīs" were a stage direction,
with all its verbs in the present tense. What would be the form and

meaning of *erat* (line 1), *solēbant* (line 2), *sedēbat* (line 3), *stābat* (line 4), etc?'

2 'Look at the last paragraph of "epistula Cephalī" and using your knowledge of verb endings work out the Latin equivalent of: "he wrote", "we handed over", "they ordered", "you (s.) prepared", "you (pl.) compelled", etc.' This kind of exercise, which asks pupils to generate Latin from English, calls for careful judgement by the teacher; if it is within the capabilities of the class it can provide useful consolidation, but if they cannot handle the transformations confidently it may be counter-productive.

3 An oral exercise based on the Language Information pamphlet, p. 14. Say, for example, 'Look at the imperfect tense of *portō* and pick out the form that means "we were carrying" ' or the reverse 'Look at the perfect tense of *doceō* and tell me the meaning of *docuistī*.' This may be followed by paragraph 2 on p. 15 and further examples on the same lines.

4 Look again at paragraphs 2–5 of the Notes at the beginning of Part Two of the Language Information pamphlet, pp. 28–9. This could be followed by asking pupils to look up the entry for e.g. *discēdō*, check its meaning and then translate various inflexions, e.g. *discēdit, discēdēbant*.

The background material

The *haruspicēs* belonged to a priestly *collēgium* dating from Etruscan dominance at Rome. Their name means literally 'those who look at entrails' and like the augurs they practised a discipline which purported to reveal the future. Their collegium at Rome consisted of sixty members. We also know that they were active at some religious centres in the provinces, for example at Nemausus (Nîmes) in southern France and Bath in Britain, and probably at other centres as well.

Lower than the haruspices on the social scale were the *astrologī*, *mathematicī*, and *Chaldaeī* who made a living, illegal at this time, out of the superstitions of ordinary people (see also the Unit IIB Handbook, pp. 73–4). For an amusing example see Pliny (*Letters* II.20) where he tells the story of Regulus, a notorious legacy hunter, who induced Verania to change her will in his favour by consulting a conveniently friendly haruspex.

The respect popularly accorded to diviners and soothsayers reflects something of the Romans' belief about the future. They believed that it cast a shadow before itself which could be recognised by the use of correct religious techniques; thus some precautions could be taken to avoid misfortune or at least to mitigate its consequences. This magical prescience was clearly widespread and by no means confined to the illiterate. Probably closely linked with it was a sense of the volatility of *fortūna*. A man could be ruler one day and a slave the next. Hence the importance of recognising the shadow of danger and avoiding it as far as possible. Some of the educated, of course, were sceptical and tended to poke fun at soothsayers; nevertheless, in varying degrees the Roman world found comfort or guidance in the words of those who read the stars, watched the flight of birds or gazed at markings on the entrails of slaughtered animals.

The different areas of the liver (p. 54) were under the influence of different gods. This bronze model was possibly used as a teaching aid.

The life-size gilded bronze head of Minerva (p. 57) was found in 1727. The unfinished top of the head suggests that the goddess probably was wearing a detachable helmet. The statue to which it belonged may well have been the cult statue of the temple.

When discussing the official religion of Rome, emphasise its ritual character and public purposes. The cult, with its apparatus of temples, sacrifices and colleges of priests, was concerned first and foremost to secure the goodwill of the gods for the state and the safe outcome of public enterprises from the beginning of a war to the building of a new town. It sought to bind together the *rēspūblica* with its divine guardians. Piety was the duty of respect owed by the citizen to these protecting powers. This formal character does not necessarily imply the absence of fervour; at religious festivals there was probably much excitement and a sense of involvement for the individual worshipper.

A more personal experience was available from other sources: firstly the continuation in rural communities of the old rituals that linked the individual to his family, the land and its guardian spirits; and secondly the mystery religions and new cults from Greece and the Middle East that expressly addressed the individual. The worship of Mithras, described in Stage 32, was one of these faiths; another was Isis worship, described in Stages 17–19 and Unit IIB Handbook, pp. 54, 60–1, 69–72. From Greece came the orgiastic rites of Dionysus and the mysteries of Demeter. Evidence of these faiths, existing in parallel with the state religion, is to be seen at many places, for instance, the temple of Isis at Pompeii and the temples of Mithras in London and on Hadrian's Wall.

By the first century the Roman world had developed a great variety of religious practice and the official attitude was one of tolerance, except where, as in the case of Christianity, the religion was felt to be politically subversive. This diversity is comparable to the wealth of religions in modern multi-ethnic societies. For further material on Roman religion see Ferguson, Ogilvie, Birley, *Life* 136–51, and Lewis and Reinhold II.552–68.

Suggestions for discussion

1 Consider why many Romans placed trust in divination.

2 Discuss with the class the prevalence of superstition, and compare Roman with modern superstitions.

3 Remind pupils of the *larārium* in Caecilius' house depicted in Filmstrip 1, frame 6 and discuss possible reasons why he had the scenes of the earthquake of A.D.62 carved upon it. Then expand the point to include votive offerings which took many different forms, e.g. the objects, perhaps an oar, perhaps articles of clothing, hung up on a temple wall by the survivors of shipwrecks.

Suggestion for further work

If a visit to an appropriate site can be arranged, e.g. Bath, Chester, Lullingstone Villa, ask pupils to look especially for any evidence of religious belief and practices at the site and to record them for discussion afterwards.

STAGE 24: FUGA

Synopsis

Reading passages ⎫
Background material ⎰ travel and communication

Language notes *cum* with subjunctive
3rd person singular and plural, imperfect and pluperfect subjunctive

in itinere

The action in both the 'high life' and 'low life' stories now leaves Bath and moves north. A short story, instead of the usual model sentences, brings back Modestus and Strythio. They are en route to Chester (where the comically incompetent performance of their duties will provide the theme of Stage 25). The new language feature is the use of *cum* with the pluperfect subjunctive, meaning 'when' or 'after'.

The reading should begin with a brief discussion of the picture. Pupils rarely fail to decide correctly which rider is which, though some may be surprised by the unglamorous figure of Modestus. The two soldiers are not travelling in uniform, but the *pugiō* and the *gladius* are visible as are the bedding-rolls and cooking-pot at the horse's tail.

A possible sequence would be: (1) lines 1–3, teacher reads aloud, asks comprehension questions, calls for translation; (2) lines 4–9, teacher reads aloud, pupils look over in pairs, teacher calls for translation; (3) lines 10–13, teacher reads aloud, pupils look over individually, teacher calls for translation. During this phase no comment should be made about the new form of the verb; comprehension questions will elicit 'when' as the meaning of *cum* and 'had come' for *vēnissent*.

Discussion of the new feature might begin as soon as the story has been read, or the teacher may prefer to leave it until after the next story, giving pupils the opportunity to meet more examples. Begin by asking pupils to pick out all the verbs in lines 1–3. Confirm that *vēnissent* is indeed a verb and a part of *venīre*, and that this new form may be identified by the -*iss*- which is a regular feature of it. Invite pupils to find other examples. By further questioning also elicit that it may be translated by 'had ...' (confirm that it is a pluperfect tense), that *cum* means 'when' in this situation and that the endings -*isset* and -*issent* are respectively the 3rd person singular and 3rd person plural. If pupils offer 'they came' for *vēnissent*, the teacher should accept this at first but by the end of the stage press for the pluperfect 'they had come'. At a convenient moment the label 'subjunctive' should be introduced but at first simply as a means of distinguishing this from other parts of the verb.

The next step is to associate in pupils' minds the conjunction *cum* with the subjunctive verb. This may be done by questioning on the lines of: 'All the sentences that have a verb in the subjunctive also have another feature. What is it?' Confirm that it is the presence of *cum* that 'causes' the subjunctive to be used. If asked, 'Does *cum* meaning "when" always lead to a subjunctive?' it is probably best to say, 'Not always, but usually; you won't meet exceptions to this rule for some time'.

Some pupils may be worried about the two uses of *cum* ('when' and 'with'). If so, point out that the easiest way to decide which is which in a particular sentence is to look at the sentence as a whole. Demonstrate with examples, e.g. *rēx cum Quīntō ambulābat* and *cum Modestus dēcidisset Strȳthiō rīsit*.

Some pupils may also ask at this point 'Why does Latin have the subjunctive? What does it mean?' For suggestions about the teacher's response, see under 'First language note', page 35 below.

Quīntus cōnsilium capit

In this and the next story the characters take sides in a way that cuts across ethnic and national boundaries: a Briton and a Roman (Dumnorix

and Quintus) try to outwit a second Briton and a second Roman
(Belimicus and Salvius). Encourage pupils to reflect on the motives for the
behaviour of all these men. What reasons, for example, would Dumnorix
have for trusting Quintus? Why should Salvius wish to bring a charge of
treason against Cogidubnus? Do you think that Quintus' motives for
wanting to protect the king are based on personal friendship or is a
principle at stake? Why should Quintus believe that an appeal to Agricola
might be effective? Is Quintus aware of the Emperor's involvement? Is he
justified in stealing horses from Salvius, his former host?

When discussing the questions on p. 63 of the pupil's text, note that in
question 4 Dumnorix has in mind not only Quintus' seizing the poisoned
cup (Stage 21) but also his killing the bear (Stage 16).

After the story has been read, the sentence *rēx . . . dē vītā suā dēspērat*
(lines 13–14) may be a suitable place for discussing the meaning of *suus*
and its contrast with *eius* and *eōrum*. Begin by putting the sentence on the
board, then write up e.g. *Cogidubnus aegrōtat. medicus dē vītā eius dēspērat.*
Have it translated and put the translation on the board. Then ask the
question, 'Both sentences translate as "despairs of his life", yet the Latin
uses a different word for "his" in each case. Can you suggest why?' When
reading Latin as opposed to translating into Latin from English there is
usually no difficulty about this point but it should be brought to pupils'
attention.

For language work, here and in the next three stages, consolidate the
morphology of the noun, particularly the genitive and dative cases, in
readiness for the introduction of the ablative without a supporting
preposition in Stage 28. A convenient form of oral practice is the
'question-per-line': select one noun in each line and ask pupils to identify
its meaning, number and case. Then, with the Language Information
pamphlet open (pp. 4–6), ask pupils which of the paradigm nouns it
resembles. Exercises of this kind should always be done with a text that
has already been read and discussed.

Another language feature requiring continued regular attention is the
participle. Ask pupils to pick out participles, link each with the correct
noun or pronoun and translate the whole phrase, and then say whether
they are present, perfect active or perfect passive.

First language note (cum with the pluperfect subjunctive)

When going through the final paragraph encourage pupils to comment on
the morphology of the pluperfect subjunctive in contrast to the 'ordinary'
(indicative) form. The paragraph has been constructed to help pupils
perceive this contrast themselves; the teacher's contribution is to confirm
and underline it.

At some point in this stage the question is likely to be asked, 'Why have a subjunctive?' or 'What does the subjunctive mean, if we can translate *trāxisset* exactly like *trāxerat?*' To this question there may be no answer that is simultaneously true, adequate and intelligible to the school pupil. Some answer may have to be attempted, but it is not the pupil's most pressing need here. To render the clause *cum . . . advēnisset* into English and to identify *advēnisset* as a verb in the 3rd person singular are the priorities. Next, as suggested above, pupils should be guided to the term 'subjunctive' as a label that distinguishes this from other parts of the verb. Thereafter, the question about the 'meaning' of the subjunctive may be approached on these lines: 'The subjunctive was used originally for things like wishes, prayers and possible rather than actual events, as in the English expressions "Let's go out", "It may rain tomorrow". The Latin subjunctive continued to have this meaning, but it also came to be used in other situations; one was in clauses with *cum.*'

Salvius cōnsilium cognōscit

By torturing Quintus' slave Salvius discovers what Quintus and Dumnorix are up to and sends Belimicus in pursuit.

Brutality towards slaves was portrayed in Stage 13. Here, when arrested for questioning about his master's disappearance, Quintus' slave is tortured as a matter of routine. Torture as a means of gaining information from slaves was practised freely in the Roman world. In fact, evidence given by slaves in court was admissible only if it had been obtained in this way.

Pupils may be invited to comment under two headings: (1) the practical reasons for torturing a slave during an enquiry, and (2) the morality of such treatment. The first will probably elicit comments on the lines of 'A good slave would be loyal to a good master such as Quintus and keep silent unless forced to reveal what he knew', or 'If a slave is tortured he is more likely to say what he thinks the torturer wants to hear.' The Romans tended to believe that statements made voluntarily, especially by a slave, were inherently unreliable. Pupils could be invited to comment. How much more reliable would evidence given under duress be than voluntary statements from different sources? Was such evidence any less dictated by self-interest?

By this point comments about the morality of torture are likely to have cropped up, expressed variously but probably tending towards belief in the value of persons and a moral obligation not to do them violence or injustice. Teachers might probe this position with questions such as: 'Does it make any difference that slaves were not regarded by Roman law as persons but as property owned by their masters?' In discussions of this sort the teacher's role is principally to keep the talking open, offer clarification of a point, help pupils listen to each other and encourage the habit of reflecting on reasons.

The notion of *auctōritās* appears in line 33 and is worth considering. Teachers might ask first 'Who is *ego*?' and 'Who is *ille*?'; then 'Do you think Salvius' claim is true? Why would he expect to have more influence with Agricola than Quintus? Because he is older? Holds a more important position? Is a friend of the Emperor?' This could lead to an analysis of Belimicus' behaviour. He could not have acted as he did without the *auctōritās* of a powerful Roman behind him.

Salvius himself is anxious only about the possible failure of his plan. About the morality of his actions he has no apparent qualms.

Second language note (imperfect subjunctive)

When taking pupils through paragraph 4, encourage them to compare the form of the imperfect subjunctive with the infinitive. Consolidation could consist of asking pupils to pick out the *cum*-clauses of the preceding story, translate them and identify the tense of the subjunctive.

Manipulation exercises

Exercise 1   Type: vocabulary
            Linguistic feature being practised: negatives
In addition to observing the Latin negative prefixes in these examples (*n(e)-, in-, dis-*), the teacher should draw attention to the English forms, both those that are the same (n-, in-, dis-) and those that differ (-less, un-). The exercise could also be used to introduce the notion of assimilation (without using the term). Ask the class, 'If *īnsānus* and *dissentīre*, why not *inpatiēns* and *disfacilis*?' If the question gets no response, invite them to try saying it and contrast that with the ease of pronouncing *impatiēns* and *difficilis*. It would be inappropriate to go further into the rules of assimilation but simple discussion of this kind may be helpful in paving the way for later work on compound verbs.

Exercise 2   Type: substitution
            Linguistic feature being practised: oblique cases of *is*,
                introduced in Stage 20
This exercise makes the incidental point that 'them' or 'it' in English may represent any gender of the pronoun in Latin. Sentences 7 and 8 may also be used orally to practise the relative pronoun. The most difficult part of the manipulation of the relative, viz. the case of the pronoun itself, should be easier since pupils will have just performed the same manipulation with *is*. For a further exercise see Language Information pamphlet, p. 13.

Exercise 3   Type: completion
              Missing item: adjective
              Criterion of choice: morphology
              Linguistic feature being practised: agreement of noun and
                  adjective, introduced in Stage 14
Examples are restricted to nominative and accusative cases, singular and
plural. Some examples contain a noun and adjective of different
declensions and different endings.

Exercise 4   Type: sentence composition from pool of Latin words
              Linguistic features being practised: nominative, accusative
                  and dative, singular and plural; present tense

The background material

Teachers are referred to Balsdon, *Life* 224–43, for a very full account of
travel in the Roman world illustrated by numerous anecdotes, to Paoli
228–31, for details of travelling vehicles, and to Casson, *Travel*.

   The Roman road system took its official starting-point from the
mīliārium aureum or 'golden milestone', probably in the form of a polygonal
column set up by Augustus in the forum and inscribed with place names
and distances. The main roads (*viae pūblicae, viae mīlitārēs*) were
constructed, owned and maintained by the state. Commissioners (*cūrātōrēs
viārum*) appointed by the emperor were responsible for the network of
main roads; smaller roads were provided and controlled by local
magistrates, with local landowners contributing to the cost of
maintenance. There were also some private roads.

   Our knowledge of this road system comes from various sources:
1 the archaeological remains of the roads themselves including milestones
   and other monuments inscribed with distances and directions. This
   evidence provides a fairly complete picture of the methods of
   construction used (see, for example, filmstrip 3). For an account of road
   building see Chevallier 82–93;
2 aerial photography, which has much increased our knowledge of the
   network where there are no physical remains on the surface. Pupils may
   need help in interpreting the photograph on p. 71 of their text (see fig. on
   p. 38). Point out the inverted T-shape of the dry valley and the folds in the
   steep slope. They may be confused by the signs of (modern) ploughing on
   the fields. This bit of road is just south of Old Sarum in Hampshire.
There are also three documentary sources for roads:
3 the *Antonine Itinerary*, compiled at the end of the second century A.D.,
   which gives details of the towns and stopping-places and the distances
   between them, along most of the main roads and some minor ones all
   over the empire;

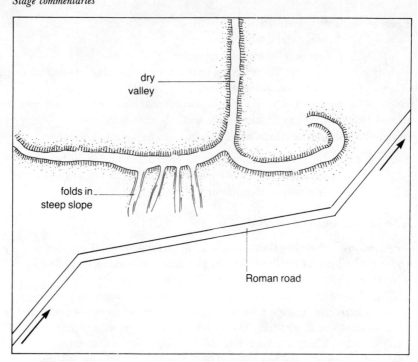

dry valley

folds in steep slope

Roman road

4 the *Peutinger Table*, a medieval copy of an ancient road map drawn in diagram form and covering the whole empire. The parts relating to Britain and Spain are unfortunately lost;
5 the *Jerusalem Itinerary* of the fourth century A.D., which shows the route from Bordeaux to Jerusalem via Arles, Milan, Istanbul and Antioch.

So far as Britain is concerned the network has been well documented by Margary. See also the very useful Ordnance Survey map of Roman Britain.

Sea travel was often quicker and easier, especially in the Mediterranean, than the lengthy overland routes, and for that reason was frequently preferred, season and weather permitting. Merchant shipping was controlled by corporations of ship-owners (*nāviculāriī marīnī*) who were responsible to superintendents appointed by the emperor. Much of their business was concerned with keeping Rome supplied with corn and they were well paid by the state for their services.

Inland waterways were also important parts of the system. Again we find corporations of merchants and barge-owners in control, making extensive connections across the empire from one waterway to another, such as the rivers Rhine, Moselle and Danube. More detailed information may be obtained from Casson, *Ships*.

Suggestions for discussion

1   Consider the various ways in which a relatively efficient road and
maritime system could affect life in the provinces, using concrete examples
wherever possible: for instance, economic influence (luxury pottery made
in southern Gaul was transported and sold across western Europe; wine,
oil and garum were exported from Campania in large quantities; the
palace at Fishbourne clearly used imported materials and craftsmen);
political and military influence (governors, administrators and troops
could reach their provinces quickly, keep the emperor informed by means
of the *cūrsus pūblicus* and put his policies into action without delay, cf.
Pliny, *Letters* X); religious influence (see *Acts of the Apostles*, e.g. 14, 17,
18.1–11, 19.21–7; and 27–8 for Paul's journey from Caesarea to Rome);
private communication and travel (there was no public postal service for
private mail. The usual procedure was to send a slave or to wait until a
friend or friend's slave was going in the right direction, cf. St Paul's
letters, e.g. 2 *Timothy* 4.9–13). Urgent letters could be sent at some expense
by special courier, cf. Pliny, *Letters* III.17; VII.12.
2   Why did people travel in the ancient world? How do the reasons
compare with reasons for travelling today? Many well-to-do inhabitants of
Rome (then as now) moved out during the summer to country villas or the
coast. Travel could also be undertaken in search of health. Thus Pliny
sent his slave Zosimus first to Egypt, then to Forum Iulii (*Letters* V.19).
Consider also, of course, the visits to Bath and other spa towns.

Words and phrases checklist

These checklists provide opportunities to consolidate vocabulary work
done in the first exercise of each stage. For example, ask pupils the
meaning of *perfidē*, *audācter* and *oppugnātor*, thereby consolidating the points
practised in Stages 21, 22 and 23 respectively.

Suggestions for further work

1   Obtain copies of the *Peutinger Table* (reproduced in Cunliffe, *Rome*)
and invite the class to find their way around the empire with its aid. A
conventional wall-map can be used in conjunction with the *Table*.
2   Get the class to calculate approximate distances and journey times
over various routes, using different means of transport. This activity could
usefully begin by looking at examples quoted in Lewis and Reinhold
II.148 and 198–207. The class might use the information on pp. 70–3 and
the map on p. 146 to estimate the length of time taken on the various
journeys mentioned in this stage: Modestus and Strythio travelling on

horseback from Bath to Chester; Salvius' slave carrying a letter to
Agricola in (perhaps) Perthshire, probably using the cursus publicus;
Quintus and Dumnorix, on horseback, trying to get from Bath to Scotland
without being captured but only reaching Chester; Belimicus and the
cavalry in pursuit of Quintus and Dumnorix.

STAGE 25: MĪLITĒS

Synopsis

Reading passages } the Roman army
Background material

Language notes   indirect question
                       1st and 2nd persons singular and plural,
                              imperfect and pluperfect subjunctive

Title picture

This shows three members of the Roman army in their uniforms. On the
left is a centurion, holding his vine-staff of office. In the middle is an
ordinary legionary in armour and with his shield, sword and javelin,
ready for battle. On the right is an *aquilifer*, wearing a bearskin and
holding the eagle, or standard, of the legion.

Model sentences

The pictures establish the scene, which is the legionary fortress at Chester
during its occupation by the Second Legion (*c.* A.D.76 to 87). Notice in
passing the turf-and-timber rampart and wooden granary of this period.
Vercobrix, son of the chief of the Deceangli, is found inside the fort,
lurking near the granary. He is arrested. The Deceangli were a tribe who
occupied the northern parts of what are now Clwyd and Gwynedd in
north-east Wales.

    After reading the model sentences, or perhaps after 'Modestus custōs',
attention may be drawn to the new feature: indirect question. Put
examples of both direct and indirect questions, selected from the model
sentences, in two columns on the board like this:

    '*quis es?*'   *mīles rogāvit quis esset.*
    '*quid prope horreum facis?*'   *iuvenis dīcere nōlēbat quid . . . faceret.*

Have them translated, then invite comment. Pupils are likely to pick out concrete points such as the absence of a question mark or quotation marks or the presence of a verb such as *rogāvit*. Take the matter a little further by asking, e.g., 'What do the examples in the right-hand column have in common compared with those on the left?' Encourage comments on the lines of 'The sentences on the right talk about or describe the questions on the left', or 'The questions on the left are as they would be in dialogue whereas the sentences on the right might be in a narrative.'

The only new word is *castra*.

Strȳthiō

The Romans have now detained Vercobrix in the gaol of the fortress. They may be less concerned with punishing his misdemeanour than with holding him as a pawn for future negotiations.

In line 1 the phrase *Strȳthiōnem . . . regressum* is a useful example of participial agreement. After the story has been read, put the phrase on the board and ask the class: 'Who has returned, the optio or Strythio? How does the Latin show this?' Then consider suitable translations, including the use of a relative clause which would produce 'He sees Strythio who has now returned to the fort.'

In line 8, if pupils offer 'I am sent' for *missus sum*, guide them towards 'I have been sent' by asking for an alternative that better fits the context. The perfect passive indicative will appear in full in Stage 30.

Some suggested questions

What tone of voice do you detect in the optio's *mī Strȳthiō, . . . mē audīre*? Ask for the sentence to be read aloud, with a suitably sarcastic effect in *quamquam occupātissimus es*.

Why do you think the Romans are keeping Vercobrix in gaol? What use might he be to them later? Can you think of similar tactics that are sometimes used in the modern world?

When Strythio says *ad statiōnem prōcēdimus* (line 32), what does he mean? From what you know of Modestus and Strythio how well do you expect them to carry out their duties?

The legionary helmet on p. 79 is bronze and the standard type of the 1st century A.D. The brow ridge on the right protected the nose and eyes and the flap on the left protected the neck. The sides of the face were protected by cheek-pieces (see drawings on pp. 75–7) which are missing here.

The dagger and its sheath-frame below are iron. The frame would have been covered with leather. The dagger was worn on the left side where it was too small to interfere with the shield arm. It was used as a knife and as a substitute for the sword if that was lost in battle.

Filmstrip 32 (slide II.54) shows a model of a legionary complete with armour and weapons.

Modestus custōs

At the gaol Modestus and Strythio take up their duties. Modestus is here at his least attractive, by turns a liar, a bully, a coward. Pupils are sometimes affronted by the slapstick. But the farce may be made more acceptable if one refers to the tradition of comic duos, for instance Morecambe and Wise or Laurel and Hardy. In Classical literature the models for Modestus and Strythio are Pyrgopolynices and Artotrogus in Plautus' *Miles Gloriosus*. Without revealing the sequel in 'Modestus prōmōtus' teachers may hint that *fortūna* will control the outcome.

Several further instances of *cum* and the pluperfect subjunctive are present. Notice also the newly introduced indirect question in, e.g., *cognōvit ubi Vercobrix iacēret* (lines 4–5), *nesciēbat enim cūr Modestus clāmāret* (lines 22–3), *rogāvit quid accidisset* (lines 29–30).

The presence of several participles should be exploited for further oral practice, by asking pupils to identify them, link each with the correct noun and translate the whole phrase. It is important to keep up this form of exercise until they are thoroughly accustomed to participles.

A useful further consolidation of the noun is to consider the different possibilities of, for instance, the *-ae* endings. The present story contains examples of *-ae* nominative plural, *etiam arāneae eum adiuvant* (lines 27–8) and of *-ae* genitive singular, *in angulō cellae iacēbat Vercobrix* (line 16). Teachers can make up further examples, always using complete sentences. One benefit is to confirm to pupils that in practice they will experience little difficulty in distinguishing these endings when they look at the meaning of the sentence as a whole.

The sword in its scabbard on p. 80 is the standard legionary sword. The Romans were trained to use their swords to stab or thrust at their enemies rather than to slash at them. This not only is a more efficient way of inflicting fatal wounds but also does not leave the right side exposed to the enemy.

First language note (indirect question)

An explanation of the distinction between direct and indirect speech is provided in paragraph 2, but encourage pupils to express it in their own words. In the final paragraph ask which are direct questions and which indirect. It is a good idea sometimes to ask pupils, after they have correctly translated an indirect question, to reconstruct in English the original direct question. Examples 7 and 8 in this paragraph may be used to show that in this construction the tense of the subjunctive is also the correct tense for translation.

Modestus perfuga

The incompetence of Modestus and Strythio has predictable results. The passage is quite easy and should be read quickly. Comprehension questions may take the place of translation throughout. At the end invite the class to close their books and listen to the cassette-recording or while the teacher reads aloud. Alternatively the class might read the passage aloud after preliminary discussion of atmosphere and points requiring emphasis.

If pupils have difficulty with *mihi fugiendum est* (I, line 18), remind them of *nōbīs festīnandum est* or *nōbīs effugiendum est* which were encountered in Stage 24. A language note on the gerundive appears in Stage 26.

Second language note (1st and 2nd persons, singular and plural, imperfect and pluperfect subjunctive)

Make sure that pupils distinguish accurately between the two tenses. Useful drills are (1) asking for tenses to be identified after reading a story and (2) asking pupils to sort out a jumbled list of verbs in both tenses and in a variety of persons. Further practice may be devised in the form of a substitution exercise, using sentences from the stories and changing the third person into the first or second person of the subjunctive, together with any other necessary changes; then ask for a translation of the altered sentence.

Manipulation exercises and further practice

Exercise 1   Type: vocabulary
                     Linguistic feature being practised: nouns with masculine/
                         feminine contrast
The exercise may be extended into some oral practice of English derivatives e.g. *captīvus/captīva* producing 'captive', 'captivate'; *fīlius/fīlia* producing 'filial', 'affiliate'. Finally ask pupils to produce the masculine equivalents of the feminine nouns in the last group, in both Latin and English. Leave *rēgīna* to last.

Exercise 2   Type: completion
                     Missing item: verb

Criterion of choice: sense

Linguistic feature being practised: forms of perfect tense

The phrases *coquum occupātum* (*invēnit*) and *Modestum īrātum vīdit* are likely to produce 'found the busy cook' and 'saw angry Modestus'. Encourage the predicative versions 'found the cook busy' and 'saw Modestus was angry'.

Exercise 3   Type: transformation

Linguistic feature being practised: nominative and dative, singular and plural

Before asking pupils to do this exercise on their own (with the aid of the Language Information pamphlet) work some examples on the board so that the steps of the transformation will be clearly understood. The last sentence may cause difficulty.

Exercise 4   Type: completion

Missing item: *cum*-clause

Criterion of choice: sense, based on 'Modestus custōs'

Exercise 5   Type: completion

Missing item: adjective

Criterion of choice: morphology

Linguistic feature being practised: agreement of noun and adjective

Incidental practice: *crēdō, pāreō* + dative

The examples are restricted to accusative and dative, singular and plural. If pupils query the word order in sentence 7, they may be told that the first position in a sentence is emphatic. English as well as Latin uses emphatic position to stress a point. Thus this sentence might be translated as 'New dresses – that's what the woman was buying.'

The background material

The life and work of the Roman soldier provide a new topic for study and one which often stimulates considerable interest.

When they look at the diagram on p. 90, pupils sometimes ask why there were not 100 men in a 'century', since the term is obviously connected with *centum*. Originally there were, but with natural fluctuation the term lost its strict numerical significance and just denoted one of the 60 divisions of the legion, each commanded by a centurion. By the beginning of the Empire, this had been standardised to about 80 men. The change in the First Cohort from six centuries of 80 men (= 480) to five centuries of 160 men (= 800) took place in the A.D.80s. The terms at the bottom of the diagram are defined on p. 94 of the pupil's text.

The quotation about recruitment also on p. 90 of the pupil's text is from Vegetius I.7.

The duty roster on page 95 of the pupil's text should be interpreted and discussed. There is considerable doubt about many of the readings and disagreement among scholars about what the abbreviations stand for and mean. The entries given in the pupil's text mainly follow the interpretations given by Watson. According to these:

C. Julius Valens was to spend 1 October training in the arena, 2 October on guard duty in the fortress tower, 3 October on drainage fatigue (e.g. digging the drains?), 4 October working on (i.e. repairing?) boots, 5 and 6 October on duty in the armoury (either guarding it or maybe maintaining the weapons), 7 October on baths fatigue, 8 October working as orderly (servant) to one of the officers, 9 October in his own century (on guard duty?) and 10 October on baths fatigue again.

L. Sextilius Germanus was to spend 1 October on guard at the gate, 2 October guarding the standards, 3 October on baths fatigue, 4 October on guard in the tower and 5–10 October on duty with D. Decrius' century.

M. Antonius Crispus was to spend 1 October on baths fatigue, 2 October on stretcher duty, 3 October in his own century, 4 October in plain clothes (perhaps civil police duties), 5 October in his own century again and 7 and 8 October acting as a tribune's escort.

T. Flavius was to spend 4, 5 and 6 October on baths fatigue and 7 October on guard at the gate.

M. Domitius was to be away from 3 October at the granaries in Neapolis (a suburb of Alexandria).

Suggested activities

This subject area is suitable for small group research (i.e. four or five pupils work together on a topic; each group reports its findings to the class and/or produces a display). For teachers on short courses this approach also has the attraction of economising on time. Groups could be asked to investigate a selection of the following:
(a) the main items of protective equipment worn by a Roman legionary soldier;
(b) the legion on the march and what it did at the end of the day's march;
(c) the arrangement of a legion on the battlefield;
(d) rewards, decorations and punishments in the Roman army (Watson is very helpful here);
(e) the deployment of the Roman army, either over the whole empire or in Britain, could be studied with maps showing the location of fortresses, the smaller forts and frontier defences;

(f) Hadrian's Wall: its construction, purposes, manning, and something of the events that affected it. Include the civilian population that lived close to the forts (pupils should be reminded, however, that Hadrian's frontier was not constructed until the second century);

(g) the *auxilia*: how they differed from the legions (different citizen status, more emphasis on cavalry, different style forts, different tasks, links with the legions). See note on *tribūnus mīlitum*, page 50 below, and filmstrip 33 (slides II.59, 60).

To supplement the information contained in this and the next two stages the following material will prove useful (for details of books, filmstrips and slides, see Bibliography on pp. 91–6).

1 Slides of military installations, e.g. Hadrian's Wall (filmstrip 35), Chester (filmstrip 30, slide II.56), York, military roads (filmstrip 3).

2 Drawings of Roman soldiers or photographs of military tombstones showing details of uniform and equipment (filmstrip 32–3; slides II.54, 59, 60). These may also be found in: Watson; Webster, *The Roman Army*; Times Newspapers wallchart; Cambridge School Classics Project, *The Romans discover Britain*; photographs of Trajan's Column in Richmond.

3 Ground plans of forts of various types and sizes; also some aerial photographs. Sources include: Van der Heyden and Scullard; Webster, *The Roman Imperial Army*; Birley, *Life*; Frere and St Joseph.

4 A selection of military inscriptions. *R.I.B.* is the definitive collection for Roman Britain but a valuable and less expensive alternative is Lactor No. 4. Both contain translations of the inscriptions quoted.

Suggestions for discussion

1 The self-sufficiency of the Roman legion and the very high proportion of fighting troops to support troops compared with the corresponding proportion (1:8) in Allied armies in World War II. Pupils might be invited to comment on reasons for this difference (e.g. the greater need for specialised support skills as military technology becomes more complex – tanks, aircraft, missiles, transport vehicles and systems of communication; compare this with the relative simplicity of first-century equipment and tactics).

2 The mixture of professional soldiers and 'amateur' commanders. Teachers can point to the value of having an army led by a man whose previous career had not been purely military but would normally have included a wider experience of law, politics and government. Other points to be made or elicited: a *lēgātus legiōnis* would not be wholly devoid of military experience since he would have served previously as a *tribūnus* (and men such as Agricola took their military tribuneship very seriously); the senior centurions played a crucial role in assisting and advising the

commander; the legatus would already have demonstrated ability to lead and organise in the civilian offices he had held.

3   The part played by the legions and auxiliary units in preserving the frontiers of the empire (most of them were stationed in the frontier provinces) and in maintaining or changing the central political power in Rome, i.e. the emperor. At the death of one holder of the principate the next claimant, especially if the successor had not been identified in advance, relied upon the support of the military to press his claims.

Words and phrases checklist

Oral practice should include a check that pupils can cope with verbs such as *cōgere* whose different forms include major variations of spelling.

STAGE 26: AGRICOLA

Synopsis

Reading passages
Background material } Gnaeus Julius Agricola

Language notes   purpose clauses
                      gerundive of obligation (impersonal use)

Title picture

This shows Agricola addressing the troops drawn up outside the principia at Chester, as described in the first story. Behind him stands Silanus. Pupils might pick out the various office-holders standing at the front.

adventus Agricolae

In place of model sentences the stage opens with a short story introducing the new feature: purpose clauses with *ut*. The scene is the fortress at Chester, where Silanus, legate of the Second Legion Adiutrix, is expecting Agricola, the governor of the province. Agricola is greeted by the troops with a spontaneous show of enthusiasm. An impression is given of a successful general who is at the same time a popular leader. The way is thus prepared for the contrast between him and Salvius.

The story is straightforward and teachers may expect a good level of understanding as it is read aloud. Give a short time for pupil exploration, then ask comprehension questions. At the end pupils might speculate as to whether Agricola's praise is sincere or consists of standard remarks that he might make to all his legions.

After reading this and, if necessary, the following story a discussion about purpose clauses could be initiated. Put up on the board the two sentences:

> *Agricola ad tribūnal prōcessit ut pauca dīceret.*
> *omnēs tacuērunt ut contiōnem Agricolae audīrent.*

Invite comment about any feature that they have in common. The reply will probably point to the subjunctive verb. Confirm this and ask pupils to identify the subjunctives. Underline them on the board. Then ask whether either of the previously met reasons for the presence of a subjunctive applies here, i.e. *cum*-clause or indirect question. After a little thought pupils are likely to say 'no'. Confirm this and invite further comment. At this point, if not sooner, *ut* will be mentioned. Confirm that this is a reason for the subjunctive, but also encourage the class to look for a common 'idea' in the clauses *ut . . . dīceret* and *ut . . . audīrent*. The object is not to elicit the label 'purpose' but to secure any appropriate observation. Pupils sometimes say that the words with the subjunctive verb give the 'reason'. One way to orient this more appropriately is to say 'That's close. Do you mean that we could put the word "because" into the translation? If we asked "Why did Agricola march to the platform?" would the answer be "because he was saying a few words"?' Normally this will direct the suggestions closer to target.

in prīncipiīs

As he waits for the confrontation, Salvius is uneasy about his story, which is a pack of lies. He must also have been conscious that (for the first time since pupils have met him) he now has to deal with a superior. Agricola, for instance, has already held the consulship; Salvius has not yet reached that office. Agricola is of senatorial rank by birth; Salvius has had to work for it.

To begin with Agricola appears to accept without question Salvius' report of treachery by Cogidubnus. Such acceptance may surprise us, but as an administrator Agricola would not take for granted the loyalty of a client-king. He might have recalled his own experience of Boudica's revolt, A.D.60–1, when as a young *tribūnus mīlitum* he witnessed the grim realities of insurrection.

Up to this point Salvius' plan has worked. Now he crucially overplays his hand, by inviting Belimicus to corroborate his story. The British chief exaggerates so much that Agricola at last becomes suspicious and begins to ask the questions he should have asked before. But almost immediately he is interrupted by Quintus' entrance. Teachers might read the story aloud section by section, asking questions as they proceed but postponing translation until after the questions on p. 100 have been discussed. The translation, perhaps of only part of the story, could be performed as a written exercise.

When taking the class through the questions notice that:

Question 1: Salvius has changed his mind since we last saw him. Then he proposed to deal with Agricola by means of a letter only; now he has decided to come in person.

Question 3: After some reflection Agricola breaks into a passionate denunciation of Cogidubnus, *quanta perfidia . . . prō amīcō habeō* (lines 11–16). Invite pupils to summarise this speech in one sentence or, better, one word.

Question 6: Agricola is initially deceived by Salvius' story because he is predisposed to trust him in a matter that concerns Roman security. Suspicion only arises when the tale is oversold. See comment above about Agricola's experience. As far as possible elicit possible reasons for Agricola's behaviour from the class. Questions like the latter part of 6 which probe the behaviour of a character are important both in themselves and as a preparation for the time when pupils read Latin literature.

Question 8: Quintus begins by establishing his credentials, to ensure that his statement will receive the full attention of his listeners.

The linguistic complexity of sentences continues to develop in the following ways:

1 'stringing' together of subordinate clauses or participial phrases, e.g. *cognōscere voluit quot essent armātī, num Britannī cīvēs Rōmānōs interfēcissent, quās urbēs dēlēvissent* (lines 32–4);

2 'nesting' of one clause or participial phrase inside another clause, e.g. *mīlitēs, cum Agricolam castra intrantem vīdissent, magnum clāmōrem sustulērunt* ('adventus Agricolae' lines 12–13); *sollicitus erat quod in epistulā, quam ad Agricolam mīserat, multa falsa scrīpserat* (lines 3–4).

To help pupils handle these long sentences teachers are recommended sometimes to use emphatic phrasing when reading aloud, sometimes to ask questions directed at various bits of the sentence before having it translated, and in due course to consolidate by using the 'Longer sentences' section of the Language Information pamphlet.

On *id quod* and *ea quae* (three examples in this story) see page 28 above. If pupils are at home with the term 'antecedent', introduced in Unit IIB, get them to compare, e.g., *id quod Salvius dīxit* with *verba quae Salvius dīxit* and hence to see that just as *verba* is the antecedent of *quae* so *id* is the antecedent of *quod*.

First language note (purpose clauses)

What should be at the forefront of the learner's attention is the whole subordinate clause, within which the subjunctive verb is the main characteristic that suggests the sense of 'purpose' and the introductory *ut* is a useful but secondary characteristic. *ut* by itself has little meaning. It is a copula that links any of a considerable variety of subordinate clauses to the main or controlling clause. Pupils should be encouraged to regard *ut* as part of the machinery of such clauses, to be translated in any way that is suitable.

Paragraph 3 takes pupils from the standard version 'in order that' to the more important idiomatic variations. Guide pupils to use these variants, by putting on the board purpose clauses taken from stories previously read and considering alternative ways of putting them into natural English. Periodically from this point onwards pupils should be asked to pick out the subjunctives in a passage, say what tense they are and why they are subjunctive.

tribūnus

It might be interesting, when the class has reached line 5, to invite speculation about the outcome. The *bona fides* of Quintus are soon established; for Rufus is none other than the estranged son of Barbillus (see Stage 20).

It is not surprising that Salvius is anxious. He hurriedly tries to undermine the credibility of anything that Quintus may say by launching into a highly coloured account of Quintus' behaviour while staying with him. Pupils might compare his statements with their recollections of the relevant parts of Stages 14 and 21. They will readily spot the bias and distortion and may be asked what these reveal about Salvius' frame of mind. Agricola on the other hand now displays a determination to get to the truth.

On the staff of a legion there would be six *tribūnī mīlitum*, one of whom, · the senior, was usually a young man of senatorial rank, while the others were members of the equestrian order. None was a full-time, professional soldier. The senatorial tribune (*tribūnus lāticlāvius*) was performing the period of military service required at the outset of the regular *cursus honōrum*; the equestrian tribunes (*tribūnī angusticlāviī*) were probably aiming at higher posts in the imperial civil service. An equestrian tribune would already have commanded an auxiliary cohort and if competent could

expect to return to the *auxilia* to command an *āla* of cavalry. After ten
years he could be promoted to one of the equestrian prefectures, such as
commander of the fleets or of the praetorian guard, or governor of
provinces such as Judaca or even Egypt.

How seriously the young senatorial tribunes took their military duties
probably varied. Tacitus (*Agricola* 5) implies that some used inexperience
as an excuse for taking long leaves and explicitly commends Agricola for
serving a hard-working apprenticeship to military command.

Second language note (gerundive of obligation)

After taking pupils through the note teachers may ask them to turn back
to 'in prīncipiīs' and 'tribūnus' to find the example of the gerundive in
each: *tibi statim cum duābus cohortibus proficīscendum est* ('in prīncipiīs' lines
19–20) and *sī tālia fēcit, eī moriendum est* ('tribūnus', line 17). The
comparison between the two ways of expressing obligation may be
illustrated by rephrasing the examples in paragraph 3 in terms of *necesse*
and putting both on the board. Avoid examples that would require a
deponent infinitive.

The last example in paragraph 3 makes a slight advance beyond the
examples in the stories because it uses the gerundive with a noun instead
of pronoun. Watch for any signs of difficulty and be ready to offer *necesse est
omnibus servīs labōrāre* for comparison.

contentiō

Perhaps because he is angry with himself, Agricola rounds on Salvius with
some ferocity. Some readers, for all their disapproval of Salvius, may feel
grudging admiration for the way in which he launches into a counter-
attack, claiming that the real issue is not justice to an ally but the new
emperor's need of money. The politician mocks the soldier.

The situation may be interpreted in more than one way. At its simplest
it can be read as a conflict of right and wrong. But there is also the battle
of wits between two powerful men and a clash of policies towards the allies
of Rome. The personal struggle remains unfinished. Although Salvius is
effectively rebuffed for the moment, he has not necessarily forfeited his
credit with Domitian.

With older pupils the comparison might be explored further: Salvius
and Agricola are not wholly dissimilar. The ruthlessness of Salvius finds
an echo in Agricola. Salvius' contempt for provincials is reflected, if only
briefly, in Agricola's *numquam nōs oportet barbarīs crēdere* ('in prīncipiīs', lines
13–14). There is, finally, the irony of the positions adopted by the two
men. For it is the soldier who speaks for the integrity of law, while the
iūridīcus argues the claims of expediency.

The story is on the cassette.

quī in line 2 is the first instance of a connecting relative. Guide pupils to realise that a relative pronoun as the first word of a sentence is often best translated by 'he' or 'they'.

Some suggested questions

What is Agricola's mood when he sends for Salvius? Which Latin words indicate his feelings?

What does Salvius do as soon as he enters the room?

What does Agricola now say about Cogidubnus? What allegations does he make against Salvius? Which Latin words convey these allegations?

Does this criticism put Salvius on the defensive? What is the tone of his reply?

Can you sum up the speeches of the two men in one line each? Which wins the argument?

Manipulation exercises and further practice

Exercise 1   Type: vocabulary
            Linguistic feature being practised: nouns of the form *amor, timor*, etc.

Exercise 2   Type: completion
            Missing item: noun
            Criterion of choice: morphology
            Linguistic features being practised: accusative, genitive and dative, singular and plural

Sentence 6 contains *crēdō* + dative. Able pupils might be left to rely on their previous experience; less able could be referred back to Stage 25 Exercise 5 sentence 6.

Exercise 3   Type: translation from English, using restricted pool of Latin words
            Linguistic features being practised (stage number of relevant language note in brackets): direct question (11), present tense of *possum* (13), agreement of adjectives (14), pluperfect tense (16), vocative (19), imperative (19), oblique cases of *is* (20), present participle (20), neuter plural (23)

Exercise 4   Type: completion
            Missing item: noun *or* verb *or* participle
            Criterion of choice: sense and syntax
            Linguistic feature being practised: sentence structure

The following exercise, using the Language Information pamphlet, may seem complicated at first but becomes easier after one or two examples have been worked by teacher and class together. The teacher puts on the board a pair of nouns with the same inflexion but different in case and sometimes number: for instance, *puerum* and *canum*. To identify each item of the pair pupils will need to refer first to the 'Words and phrases' section to check the nominative and genitive singular of each word and then to 'About the language' to relate that information to the appropriate specimen noun on pp. 4–6. Ask pupils to work out the case (or possible cases) of each item in the pair, whether it is singular or plural and which specimen noun it is like. Include examples that contrast -*īs* with -*ĭs*; examples that contrast -*ī* (genitive singular and nominative plural of 2nd declension) with -*ī* (dative singular of 3rd declension). Some examples should be presented as whole sentences, reinforcing the point that context provides strong clues to the correct classification. For example,

> *clāmor canum puerum magnopere terrēbat.*
> *stolae mercātōris fēminīs nōn placent.*
> *strepitus urbis fēminīs Graecīs semper placēbat.*
> *servī canī cibum cotīdiē dabant.*
> *servī dē vītā Barbillī dēspērābant.*
> *mercātor vīnum caupōnum Pompēiānōrum vituperāvit.*

At the end of a story spend a few minutes on the familiar exercise of picking out items, but now extend the repertoire to include, e.g. relative clauses, adjectives and the nouns they agree with, genitive cases and the nouns they depend on. Speed and accuracy are enhanced by this sort of exercise and boost pupils' confidence and fluency of reading.

The 'About the language' section of the Language Information pamphlet offers further material for consolidation and should be used periodically during the final stages of Unit IIIA.

The background material

The inscription on the water-pipe can be translated: 'In the ninth consulship of the Emperor Vespasian and the seventh of Titus (victorious general), when Gnaeus Julius Agricola was governor of the province.'

For the other inscription, we have followed the version published in *J.R.S.* 1956 by R. P. Wright which remains the most generally accepted. Pupils may be surprised that so much of an inscription can be reconstructed with a fair degree of certainty when so little has actually survived. In this case the 'GRIC' at the bottom establishes that the inscription is about Agricola, and his official titles and the standard formulae are known from other sources. Note however that the fourth fragment shows that the reconstruction is incomplete, and in fact the purpose of the inscription has never been established. The version here may be translated:

> The Emperor Titus Caesar, son of the deified Vespasian, Vespasian Augustus, Pontifex Maximus, holding tribunician power for the ninth time, saluted as *Imperator* fifteen times, Consul for the seventh time, (Consul) designate for the eighth time, Censor, Father of the Fatherland, and Caesar Domitian, son of the deified Vespasian, Consul for the sixth time, (Consul) designate for the seventh time, Patron of the Youth, Priest of all the priestly Colleges, Gnaeus Julius Agricola being Governor of the Imperial Province ...

The pupil's text covers Agricola's career as far as his appointment as governor of Britain. Some aspects of his governorship will have emerged from the Latin stories, but teachers may wish to add a selection of the following details.

During A.D. 77 Agricola was a *cōnsul suffectus*. At this time the duration of the consulship might be as short as two months and we do not know when during the year A.D.77 Agricola was consul. This has given rise to uncertainty about the date of his arrival in Britain as governor. There are reasons (see the edition of the *Agricola* by Ogilvie and Richmond, appendix 1) for assuming that he travelled to the province in the summer of A.D.78. That this province should have been assigned to him was not surprising in view of his experience and knowledge of it. What was unusual was that he should have been permitted to govern it for 7 years.

On arrival he dealt with the Ordovices, who had ambushed a regiment of cavalry in north Wales and annexed Anglesey. His readiness to act so late in the campaigning season and so soon after arrival (Tacitus, *Agricola* 18) may indicate his familiarity with the province. In A.D.79 he began the campaigns which took Roman forces to the far north of Britain. The line of advance chosen by Agricola was probably along the western route, going north from Viroconium (Wroxeter) and Deva through Lancashire. As each tribe was defeated, it was offered 'pardon and peace', and its area was penetrated by roads and guarded by forts. A road was built between the Tyne and Solway estuaries, the shortest and most easily defensible line across the island. Within fifty years this became Hadrian's Wall and the northern frontier of the empire. Each summer campaign took Agricola further northwards until he reached southern Scotland. During the winter when the marching and fighting was brought to a stop he worked at a policy of romanisation. The native aristocracy was encouraged to adopt Roman dress, language and manners, while temples, market-places, fine houses and public baths were built.

Tacitus might be suspected of exaggerating his subject's virtues. He is, after all, writing to praise and to vindicate. But the evidence of archaeology appears to confirm Tacitus' claims. Tacitus also ascribes to him considerable personal and administrative qualities. The impression is given of a man of simple tastes, careful judgement, honest and well disposed to the native population. The rapid expansion of urban life in Britain in the second century may have owed as much to his civil policies as to his military prowess.

The battle of Mons Graupius in A.D.84 broke the final resistance of the tribes led by Calgacus. It also brought the climax and end of Agricola's public life. Recalled by Domitian, awarded triumphal honours, a statue and a citation, he nevertheless thought it wise to retire into the safety of private life. Domitian did not call on him again to lead Roman armies; and when the governorship of Asia fell vacant Agricola excused himself. Shortly afterwards he died of an illness which Tacitus hints may have been the work of a poisoner.

After the pupil's text has been studied, teachers might read to their classes from Tacitus' *Agricola* (Penguin translation) Chapter 21 (romanisation) and Chapters 33–4 (speech to troops at Mons Graupius).

Words and phrases checklist

On the importance of oral practice of the different forms of such verbs as *auferre*, see p. 36 above. *auferre* itself may be worth discussion: show its origin as *abferō, abtulī* etc. and let pupils appreciate, by experiment, the greater ease of pronunciation of *auferō, abstulī*. It is important that such variations be seen as having logical reasons.

STAGE 27: IN CASTRĪS

Synopsis

Reading passages } Background material }	Chester: the legionary fortress
Language notes	indirect command
	impersonal verbs
	result clauses

Title picture

This shows the fortress at Chester with the Welsh hills and the river Dee in the background, based on the diorama in the Grosvenor Museum, also shown on filmstrip 30 (slide II.56). The main streets in Chester today still follow the lines of the Roman ones. Pupils might use the plan on p. 123 to help them pick out important buildings.

Model sentences

The scene is now set for the dénouement of the Modestus sub-plot. In the first picture Modestus is pointing towards the granary which is the setting for the following stories.

The linguistic feature introduced is indirect command. The *oratio recta* that corresponds to each indirect command appears within the picture as an imperative uttered by one of the figures. There are two ways of approaching the model sentences: (1) begin by discussing the picture, including the imperative within it (which pupils should recognise) and then turn to the caption that contains the indirect command, or (2) proceed directly to the caption containing the indirect command and employ the picture, including the imperative phrase, as clue to the meaning. The first method may prove easier. Discussion of the formal relationship between the direct and indirect utterances may be postponed until the language note on pp. 114–15 has been reached.

Some vocabulary may cause difficulty, e.g. *contiōnem . . . habēbat*. Help pupils to infer the meaning by studying the picture. The only new word is: *imperābat*.

sub horreō

Use this and the following story to build up pupils' understanding of the fortress. Some of the questions following the passage require discussion of the setting; reading the background material will therefore be a necessary preliminary to working on them. The questions may be used in turn to introduce a wider study of the legionary fortress, including guided reading in other books. As the reading proceeds certain topics should be dealt with:

1 The design of the *horreum*. The floor was supported above ground level on rows of low pillars leaving two feet or more between the floor and the ground. Fresh air circulated in this space, maintaining dry cònditions for the foodstuffs and deterring vermin. In the first century A.D. granaries seem generally to have been built of wood; from the second century onwards, stone was normal.

2 *coquus*. Although each *contubernium* of eight men would draw daily rations and prepare its own food, probably over a charcoal fire on the verandah in front of their living quarters, a legionary fort would also be

equipped with ovens and kitchens to bake bread and cook foodstuffs
that the small fires could not cope with.

3 If pupils ask questions about dice playing, remind them of Stage 22.

4 *vīcus*. At Chester, as at many other places of military occupation, a
civilian settlement quickly grew up. There may already have been a
settlement near the site but the arrival of the army ensured that the
settlement expanded, tucked between the fort and the river, and
engaged in supplying the wants of a large, permanent garrison – fresh
food, hardware, inns and shops, social company.

Notice the build up of clauses of indirect command at the end of the
passage. The aim is to get pupils to read them with some confidence
before the language note.

The description of Strythio as *vir maximī silentiū, minimīque iocī* (lines
13–14) should stimulate idiomatic renderings. Invite the class to put
suggestions on paper for a few minutes, then compare and list the liveliest
on the board.

If pupils, when doing the first part of question 4, think that Strythio is
to bring the dinner, draw attention to *eum . . . coquere et hūc portāre* (line 21).

First language note (indirect command)

While working through this note confirm to the class that clauses of
indirect command in Latin depend not only on a verb such as *imperō*
meaning 'command' or 'order' but also and frequently on verbs such as
persuādeō, ōrō, moneō whose meanings are much less imperative. The
negative conjunction *nē* is postponed until Stage 29.

The word 'usually' at the end of paragraph 2 on p. 115 may prompt a
query. If so, pupils should be told of *iubeō* and *vetō* which control the
infinitive instead of the subjunctive. Refer to e.g. Stage 26 'tribūnus', *tē
iubeō hunc hominem summā cum cūrā interrogāre* (line 5).

In paragraph 4, ask pupils to say which sentences are direct and which
are indirect commands. As a further exercise: (1) after reading an indirect
command ask pupils to reconstruct in English the original direct
command, (2) convert a direct command into its indirect equivalent, e.g.
'*abī, Cogidubne*', *inquit Salvius* may become *Salvius Cogidubnō imperāvit ut
abīret*. This exercise, however, should only be attempted with a very able
class, working together under the teacher's guidance with the sentence
being built up on the blackboard.

When the construction has been grasped, teachers might introduce a
discussion on *sē* and *eum*. Put the sentence, *senex nōs ōrābat ut sibi parcerēmus*
(para. 4, no. 6), on the blackboard, have it translated and write the
translation beneath. Then change *sibi* to *eī* and say 'This sentence too is
translated "The old man begged us to spare him", but it doesn't mean

quite the same as the previous sentence. Can anyone suggest a
difference?'

Modestus prōmōtus

Led by Vercobrix, ten Britons head for the granary where Modestus is
waiting. Modestus, in the manner of comedy, becomes an improbable
hero.

The passage is suitable for reading aloud, and as the Latin is fairly easy
teachers might initially read it aloud in short portions, asking
straightforward comprehension questions after each portion.

Given that the story is farce, the possibilities for serious discussion of
character are limited, but at the end the teacher may usefully check that
pupils have a clear grasp of the technical terms used: *vallum* (line 4), the
defensive wall round the fortress, at that time an earth mound topped by a
stout wooden palisade. Later it was converted to a stone wall, parts of
which have survived; *horrea* (line 5), the granaries (for details see pupil's
text p. 125, and p. 56 above); *praefectus castrōrum* (lines 43–4), the
legionary officer responsible for running the camp, its administration and
supplies; *lēgātus* (line 49), the commanding officer of a legion. Agricola was
lēgātus of the Twentieth Legion in Britain, A.D.71–3. Distinguish the
lēgātus legiōnis, however, from the *lēgātus Augustī prō praetōre*, who was the
military governor of the whole province. Other technical terms met earlier
might be recalled here, e.g. *prīncipia*, the headquarters building (for details
see pupil's text p. 124).

Linguistically, the commas at the beginnings and ends of participial
phrases are now being phased out. When pupils are reading the Latin
aloud teachers should observe whether they identify these boundaries by
noticeable pauses or still appear uncertain about the beginnings and ends
of these phrases.

Near the end, two sentences appear each containing a participial
phrase: *Rōmānī Britannōs ex horreō extractōs ad carcerem redūxērunt. tum lēgātus
legiōnis ipse Modestum arcessītum laudāvit* (lines 48–50). The literal version is
such unnatural English that pupils will attempt to produce something
more natural. That should be accepted and encouraged. It will however
be useful also to put the Latin sentence on the board accompanied by a
literal version to show that grammatically *extractōs* is a passive participle in
agreement with *Britannōs*. After the analysis, go back to idiomatic English
equivalents.

Notice also that the participial phrase is itself being expanded in new
ways. In Stage 26 'in prīncipiīs' we had a dative case depending on the
participle, *hīs verbīs diffīsus* (line 31). Now there is *ē manibus Britannōrum*

ēlāpsus (line 34). In Stage 28 an important further change will appear with the attachment of a noun in the ablative without a preposition, e.g. *morbō afflīctus*.

The antefix on p. 118 is early second century and comes from the army depot at Holt near Chester. Antefixes were set at intervals along the eaves of buildings, to cover the ends of the semi-circular roof-tiles, as shown in the title picture of Stage 24 on p. 59.

Second language note (impersonal verbs)

Latin impersonal verbs are often more naturally expressed in English by a personal construction: for example, *mihi placet* becomes 'I am pleased'. This may give pupils the impression that impersonal verbs are oddities, found only in Latin. The impression may be corrected by drawing attention to familiar impersonal usages in English, e.g. 'it worries me', 'it's getting late'. Some pupils may have already remarked on the plethora of ways in Latin for expressing the notion of obligation. Again, a comparison with English will correct the impression of strangeness. Compare the English words 'ought', 'must', 'should', 'have to', 'got to', even 'need to'.

Manipulation exercises

Exercise 1   Type: vocabulary
             Linguistic feature being practised: nouns in *-tūdō*
The aim is to build up awareness of a class of abstract nouns in which the common ending *-tūdō* nominalises a qualitative adjective, e.g. *altus – altitūdō*. Pupils may be helped by a similar relationship in English, e.g. 'wide' and 'width', 'ugly' and 'ugliness', though English lacks the uniform ending.

Exercise 2   Type: completion
             Missing item: participle
             Criterion of choice: sense, syntax and morphology
             Linguistic feature being practised: present, perfect passive
                 and perfect active participles, introduced in Stages 20, 21,
                 22

Exercise 3   Type: transformation
             Linguistic feature being practised: nominative and
                 accusative singular and plural, including examples of
                 neuter singular (introduced in Unit IIB Language
                 Information pamphlet) and neuter plural (introduced in
                 Stage 23)

Exercise 4   Type: completion
            Missing item: noun ending
            Criterion of choice: morphology
            Linguistic features being practised: nominative, accusative,
                genitive and dative, singular and plural

The exercise is intended to diagnose whether more consolidation is needed
of any of these cases, in readiness for the introduction of the ablative case
(without preposition) in Stage 28. If further practice is thought desirable
it could be conducted on the lines of the exercise described above, p. 53.
Put on the board a list of nouns in various cases, singular and plural,
including some unfamiliar nouns and forms that might be one of several
cases, then ask pupils to use both sections of the Language Information
pamphlet in order to identify the cases and say which specimen noun
each example resembles.

Third language note (result clauses)

Comment on the conjunction *ut* should still treat it simply as a device to
link one part of the sentence to another. Encourage pupils to translate *ut*
according to context and the dictates of natural English.

But attention should be drawn to the anticipatory words associated
with result clauses. Gather these from the pupil's text and list them on the
board: *tam, tot, tantus, adeō*; mention also *tālis, ita*.

The background material

Chester has provided the setting for the stories in Stages 25–7. The
general information about legionary fortresses in the pupil's text might be
supplemented with some of the following details relating specifically to
Chester.

1 The site of the fortress was well chosen. It was near a river estuary and
   so could be provisioned by sea to function as a stores depot for military
   units in the area. It also stood between the mountains of north Wales,
   the hills of Derbyshire and the northern Pennines. Perhaps most
   importantly, it controlled the western route to the north.
2 The Second Legion was withdrawn from Britain perhaps for service in
   Domitian's campaigns in Dacia in about A.D.87. Its place at Chester
   was taken by the Twentieth Legion, which had been pulled back from
   Scotland when Agricola's strategy of conquering the whole island was
   abandoned by Domitian.
3 To begin with, the fortress had a turf-and-timber rampart and
   buildings constructed mainly of wood, as the drawings show, but in the
   second century it was rebuilt in stone. The later mediaeval city of

Chester grew up directly over the fortress and made it impossible for the site to be excavated as a whole. Therefore, though the general layout has been identified, many details remain obscure. However, as most legionary fortresses were built to the same pattern, our knowledge can be supplemented by evidence from other sites, e.g. Neuss in western Germany (see Webster, *The Roman Imperial Army*, pp. 183–7).

The plan of a legionary fortress in the pupil's text, p. 123, is based on Chester, with some details added from the 'standard' pattern where they have not been definitely identified in Chester. The drawing on p. 127 shows a corner of the fortress. Notice the cooking ovens against the rampart.

After pupils have read the description of the legionary fortress, discuss the activities connected with the major structures. The aim should be to imagine life within the fortress and to understand the purpose of the buildings. For instance, the ground plan of a barrack block becomes more interesting when one thinks of the eight men who lived and slept in each pair of cells with its colonnaded porch outside. Similarly, one might discuss the tribunal, the platform at one end of the basilica. From here the commanding officer dispensed military justice and may also have harangued assemblies of officers and centurions about slack discipline or the standard of weapon drill. Finally ask pupils to prepare a labelled plan to show the main features of a fortress. Large drawings could be prepared by small groups.

There is a reconstruction of a turf-and-timber fort of the period at the Lunt, Baginton, near Coventry.

Words and phrases checklist

Draw attention to and practise the perfect participle of *augeō*. It will appear in the model sentences of Stage 28.

Suggestions for further work

A project on military life in Britain could be undertaken. The work would probably best be carried out in groups of three to five pupils, using two or three consecutive lessons, if time allows.

Depending on reference material available (for suggestions, see Bibliography), and avoiding duplication of work in Stage 25, possible topics for research include:

1 the main phases of the occupation of Britain from A.D.43 to the arrival of Agricola;

2 Agricola as a military commander;

3 the history and design of a legionary fortress, e.g. Lincoln, York, Chester, Caerleon;

4 the network of military roads which were developed soon after occupation began. Why were certain routes chosen? Do they follow high or low ground? How were they surveyed and built? What traffic, apart from the military, used them? How were the roads protected?

The military material in this stage provides opportunities for pupils to draw conclusions from the evidence, whether in the course of the activities outlined above or during discussion while the stories are being read. For example:

1 Why could a soldier, perhaps just transferred from Novaesium (Neuss) in Germany, find his way around the fortress at Chester without any difficulty?

2 At the time of these stories a century contained 80 men. What do you think its original number was (see above, p. 44)?

3 Why did the Romans put the ovens at the *edge* of the fortress (see picture on p. 127) and not, for example, in the middle of the barrack blocks?

4 Why did the Romans site the principia towards the centre of the fort instead of just inside the main gate?

STAGE 28: IMPERIUM

Synopsis

Reading passages	conclusion of the Roman Britain narrative
Background material	sources of our knowledge of Roman Britain
Language notes	ablative singular and plural expressions of time prepositions

---

Model sentences

Salvius' punitive action against a farmer who resists the demand for money represents the harsher side of Roman occupation.

The ablative case, previously used only in prepositional phrases or (more recently) in expressions of time, is now used in association with a perfect passive participle, e.g. *gladiō centuriōnis vulnerātus*. The forms themselves of the ablative are already familiar, but the meanings of the new usage will need to be explored and practised.

In the last sentence on p. 131, *complētam* may cause a little difficulty. If pupils say 'complete with money' remind them of *viās complēbant*, 'they filled the streets'. With this and other instances of elusive vocabulary encourage pupils to seek clues in the pictures and make full use of the context before allowing resort to the 'Words and phrases'.

The following words are new: *extulērunt, catēnīs, abdūxērunt, timōre.*

testāmentum

This first passage takes the form of a Roman will and is important for understanding the stories that follow. Each bequest is prefaced by the formula, *dō, lēgō*, followed immediately by the name of the beneficiary and then the details of the gift (see also Barbillus' will in Stage 20, p. 82). It is worth drawing attention to the careful drafting and standard phraseology that typify a formal document and inviting comparison with similar pieces of writing in English, for example an insurance certificate or (probably more familiar to pupils) a television licence.

Cogidubnus begins by nominating the emperor as his heir. A Roman takeover after his death is inevitable and he accepts it. If, however, the opening of this will is predictable, the substance of what follows is certainly not. For it not only makes a friendly mention of Salvius, it also leaves him two silver tripods and, in the event of Dumnorix also being dead, a thousand *aureī* and the palace itself. Speculation should be aroused by this. Some pupils may suggest that after the will was given to Salvius for safe-keeping Salvius tampered with it. The teacher could then query whether Cogidubnus was likely to have entrusted his will to Salvius at all. Postpone any definite answer until the end of the next story. The will concludes with the standard formula, *dolus malus ab hōc testāmentō abestō!* Some pupils will appreciate the irony.

For the most part the language is simple and may be handled by comprehension questions, e.g. 'What legacy does so-and-so receive?', but it does contain one example of 'branching' in lines 15–16, *L. Marcius Memor, ubi aeger ad thermās vēnī, ut auxilium ā deā Sūle peterem, benignē mē excēpit*, where the clause *ut . . . peterem* branches out of the clause *ubi . . . vēnī*. Sentence patterns of this kind have occurred occasionally since Stage 18. Handle this example by reading it aloud carefully and asking questions before it is translated.

Instances of the new use of the ablative with a passive participle also occur: *morbō gravī afflīctus* (line 2), *spē praedae adductī* (line 7), *īnsāniā affectī* (line 7), *manū meā scrīptum ānulōque meō signātum* (lines 26–7).

If pupils query the use of the abbreviations *C.* and *Cn.* for *Gāius* and *Gnaeus*, point out that this is a convention, surviving from the time when the sounds of 'c' and 'g' were represented by the same symbol.

Some suggested questions

Can you suggest reasons why Cogidubnus should name the emperor as his heir in spite of the humiliation he has suffered?

Would you expect him to have bequeathed more to Agricola?

What conclusions may be drawn from the amiable references to Salvius and the legacies allotted to him? Can you recall the history of these silver tripods (see Stages 14, p. 34, and 26, p. 102)?

The will provides for the transfer of legacies from Dumnorix to Salvius, if Dumnorix dies before Cogidubnus. Notice the 'coincidence' that in the one clause where this provision is made, the first legatee (Dumnorix) has indeed died. Does this suggest anything?

Cogidubnus thanks Belimicus for saving his life in the incident with the bear, Stage 16. Was this true?

Why should Cogidubnus ask that *gemmās meās, paterās aureās, omnia arma quae ad bellum vēnātiōnemque comparāvī* (lines 24–5) be buried with him? What beliefs about the after-life are suggested by this?

in aulā Salviī

Salvius takes possession of his inheritance. In practice the way is open to him to seize control of the whole tribal area. But Belimicus is dissatisfied and embarks upon conspiracy. His supposed allies soon betray him.

As a variation from the rubric at the head of the story, the first part could be handled by getting pupils to work in pairs or small groups on the first six comprehension questions before any other work is done. The questions are straightforward and will guide exploration to the end of the third paragraph. Supplementary questions that might be asked include:

What sort of things would Salvius do *ut rēs Cogidubnī administrāret* (line 3)?

Which words give the reason why *plūrimī prīncipēs . . . Salvium adiuvābant* (line 5)?

What was the hope of Belimicus, *spē praemiī adductus* (line 6)? How did he set about achieving his ambition?

The rest of Part I could then be read in the usual way and after translation the class could turn to the last three questions. Finally some interpretation of behaviour should be attempted. Does Salvius seem to be sad or happy, anxious or confident? How have his feelings changed since he sat in the principia at Deva waiting for Agricola? What were Salvius' feelings after learning of Belimicus' conspiracy? How does Salvius show his character in the steps he takes? Considering what Belimicus had already done to assist Salvius were his ambitions reasonable?

In Part II Belimicus plunges towards disaster. A reference to receiving his deserts, *praemium meritum* (line 10) is answered by Salvius with practised irony, *praemium meritum iam tibi parāvī* (line 13); there follows a thinly veiled note of triumph in Salvius' *volō tē garum exquīsitissimum gustāre* (line 14). Failing to sense the menace in the words, Belimicus continues to dream. When Salvius makes his admission of having forged the will, reality begins to dawn.

As with Part I, the class could be invited to work through the first two paragraphs in small groups to find the answers to questions 1 and 2. Then take pupils carefully through the rest using mainly comprehension questions to keep them close to the rising tension. Translation may be postponed.

Now that it has been established that the will is a forgery, pupils might look at it again and consider why Salvius bothered to include a legacy to Agricola. Would the omission of any gift to Agricola have aroused suspicion? Was Salvius dumping an unwanted *objet d'art* on his rival?

First language note (ablative singular and plural)

In paragraph 1 the ablative case has been put in a participial phrase and translated in four out of the five examples with 'by'. This is the first step into the diversity of ways of conveying the sense of the ablative in English. If pupils ask whether other ways are acceptable, e.g. *iniūriā incēnsī* 'angered at the injustice', reply approvingly and confirm that the ablative can be handled in many ways.

In paragraph 2 teachers should demonstrate clearly the pronunciation of the ablative singular of the first declension, *puellā*, and invite pupils to state in their own words the difference between that and the nominative singular. Write more examples on the board and get the class to speak them aloud.

In paragraph 3 teachers may begin to encourage alternative versions. Thus *audāciā Belimicī attonitus* may become 'astonished by the audacity of Belimicus' or 'astonished at Belimicus' audacity' or similar.

Some pupils may notice the difference between, e.g., *pugiōne vulnerātus* (instrumental use of the ablative) and *ā Belimicō vulnerātus* (ablative with *ā* or *ab* to express the agent). If possible, however, defer discussion for another stage or two, to enable pupils to meet the ablative in varied contexts in the stories. Once they are handling it with some confidence in their reading, then the time will be opportune to draw attention formally, with the aid of examples on the board, to the distinction between agent and instrument.

Belimicus rēx

Salvius now toys with his victim and promises him a kingdom after all. He emerges from the episode an easy victor.

Clauses of result and indirect command, both recently introduced, continue to be present. Attention should be given to the way pupils are now managing the participial phrases, especially the perfect passive with an ablative noun, e.g. *hīs verbīs perturbātus* (line 16), *garum venēnō mixtum* (line 9), *spē ultiōnis adductus* (line 31) and an extension of this pattern *metū mortis pallidus* (line 22), where an adjective replaces the participle. A useful exercise consists of putting these and similar phrases on the board and having them translated orally. Encourage alternatives; e.g. *spē ultiōnis adductus* (line 31) may be rendered by 'driven by the hope of revenge', 'inspired by hopes of revenge' or simply 'in hope of revenge' or 'hoping to gain revenge'.

The skeleton on p. 141 is a mosaic from Pompeii. It carries two wine-jugs and probably came from the centre of a dining-room floor.

This story is on the cassette.

Some suggested questions

Was there a point when Belimicus might have recognised his danger and turned back to safety?

How does Salvius exploit Belimicus' greed?

Do you think Belimicus deserved his fate? If so, does this excuse Salvius? What reasons may have prompted Salvius to kill Belimicus rather than deal less severely with him?

Why, in your opinion, does Salvius succeed and Belimicus fail?

Second language note (expressions of time)

Work on this note might be prefaced by putting some sentences containing both types of time phrases on the board and inviting pupils to translate and comment. The note can thus be used as confirmation of what pupils have already deduced. Further practice can be supplied by giving some examples in English and asking whether each phrase would, in Latin, be accusative or ablative.

If during this stage or later the class does some work on Roman inscriptions, especially those of soldiers' tombstones, they will come across the use of the ablative for duration of time. This should simply be noted as a common alternative, especially in non-literary Latin.

Manipulation exercises

Exercise 1   Type: vocabulary
               Linguistic feature being practised: nouns in *-ia*

Exercise 2   Type: completion
               Missing item: clause
               Criterion of choice: sense
               Incidental practice: uses and tenses of subjunctive

Exercise 3   Type: completion
               Missing item: noun
               Criterion of choice: sense
               Incidental practice: ablative

Third language note (prepositions)

In view of the many prepositional phrases already encountered, pupils are
unlikely to have trouble with this note. Possibilities for further practice:
1 Put on the board pairs of phrases and ask for their meaning, e.g. *in urbe –
   in urbibus; sub mēnsīs – sub mēnsā; in viīs – in viā; ē vīllā – ē vīllīs; in templō – in
   templīs.* The order of singular and plural in these pairs should be varied.
2 The untranslated prepositions at the ends of paragraphs 2 and 3 could
   be put into phrases and used for revision. Do pupils remember the
   meanings?
3 Able pupils might turn such phrases as 'with the friend', 'into the
   house', 'across the bridge' into Latin. Take care to keep the vocabulary
   simple. Do the exercise orally, and using the blackboard. An extension
   to this is to ask pupils to convert singular phrases into plural and vice
   versa.

The background material

Pupils now come to the end of the sequence on Roman Britain and it
would be desirable if before moving on they looked back over this theme.
In the pupil's text the background section reviews the sources of our
knowledge and emphasises the interrelationship of the different kinds of
evidence – literary, archaeological and epigraphic.

    The first step in discussion may consist simply of recalling material
from the stories. If, for instance, slavery in Roman Britain is being
reviewed, begin by asking the class what they remember of the treatment
of the slaves they have encountered: e.g. Salvius' harsh treatment of the
labourers on his estate (Stage 13); the somewhat easier life of domestics in
his villa (Stage 14); the torture of the slave after the flight of Quintus and
Dumnorix (Stage 24).

This prepares the way for the question: how do we know that slaves were treated like this? What evidence supports the stories? Information from the background sections should be brought in here. Some pupils will remember the photograph (Stage 13, p. 7) of a slave chain, or Columella's advice (Stage 13, p. 19) to accommodate chained slaves in an underground prison. Teachers might help to build up the picture of the literary evidence by quoting from Varro's *De Re Rustica* and Columella. Translations of parts will be found in C.S.C.P. *The Roman World*, Book 7 *The Villa*, pp. 15–16.

Further topics that may be reviewed in this way include:

1 The Roman invasion of Britain (Stage 14, pp. 38–41). Evidence: Caesar, *Gallic War* IV.20–36; V.8–23 (read the Penguin translation to the class); Dio Cassius LX. 19–23; Tacitus, *Agricola* 13.

2 Cogidubnus and the palace at Fishbourne (Stages 15 and 16). Evidence: Tacitus, *Agricola* 14; archaeological excavation at Fishbourne and the Chichester inscription. The diagram on p. 151 is a stylised diagram of the stratification at Fishbourne, to show how layers can provide evidence for the occupation of a site.

3 The Roman baths and temple at Aquae Sulis (Stage 21). Evidence: Solinus, *Collectanea rerum memorabilium* 22.10; archaeological evidence including inscriptions, Roman coins and defixiones found in the spring; the Roman architecture of baths and temple.

4 The military presence, for example at Chester (Stages 25–7). Evidence: the remains of the fortress; military inscriptions, especially on tombstones (see the section on Chester reprinted from *R.I.B.* by Collingwood and Wright); also Webster, *A Short Guide to the Roman Inscriptions*; items of military equipment.

Useful sources of evidence, in addition to those cited above, are given in the Bibliography, pp. 91–4.

The map on p. 146 shows in more detail than in Stage 14 (p. 37) the early development of Roman Britain. The peaceful consolidation in the south-east (see p. 150) is clearly illustrated by the preponderance of roads, towns and villas, compared with the north and west, where legionary fortresses indicate continuing military activity. Key to Roman names:

Aquae Sulis = Bath	Isca (south-west) = Exeter
Calleva = Silchester	Lindum = Lincoln
Camulodunum = Colchester	Londinium = London
Corinium = Cirencester	Luguvalium = Carlisle
Corstopitum = Corbridge	Mona = Anglesey
Deva = Chester	Noviomagus = Chichester
Eboracum = York	Pinnata Castra = Inchtuthil
Glevum = Gloucester	Verulamium = St Albans
Isca (Wales) = Caerleon	Viroconium = Wroxeter

Inscriptions

p. 154: A slide of this inscription is obtainable from the Grosvenor
Museum, Chester. The expanded version reads:

> D(is) M(anibus) / Caecilius Avit/us Emer(ita) Aug(usta) / optio
> leg(ionis) XX / V(aleriae) V(ictricis) st(i)p(endiorum) XV vix(it) /
> an(nos) XXXIIII / h(eres) f(aciendum) c(uravit)
>
> (R.I.B. 492)

> To the spirits of the departed. Caecilius Avitus of Emerita Augusta,
> optio of the Twentieth Legion Valeria Victrix, of 15 years' service, lived
> 34 years. His heir had this set up.

Emerita Augusta was a *colōnia* in Lusitania, now Mérida in Spain. The
Twentieth Legion received the second V (Victrix) in its name in
acknowledgement of its exploits during Boudica's revolt, A.D.61.
Caecilius holds in his left hand a square tablet-case, in his right a long
staff (the optio's badge of office).

p. 155: This inscription is in the Grosvenor Museum, Chester. The
expanded version reads:

> C(aius) Lovesius Papir(ia tribu) / Cadarus Emerita mil(es) / leg(ionis)
> XX V(aleriae) V(ictricis) an(norum) XXV stip(endiorum) IIX /
> Frontinius Aquilo h(eres) f(aciendum) c(uravit)
>
> (R.I.B. 501)

> Gaius Lovesius Cadarus of the Papirian voting-tribe, from Emerita,
> soldier of the Twentieth Legion Valeria Victrix, aged 25, of 8 years'
> service. Frontinius Aquilo, his heir, had this set up.

Lovesius is a Spanish name. Emerita = Emerita Augusta.

Suggestions for further work

1 More examples of funerary inscriptions, civilian as well as military,
will be found in Filmstrip 2, frames 33–4 (slides 15–17) and in Filmstrip 3,
frames 16, 18 and 33 (slides 61–8). As noted above, other inscriptions may
be found conveniently presented and translated in Lactors No. 4 and No.
8. Working on this material should normally be a collaborative activity
between teacher and class and then by pupils in groups. If time allows,
groups may be asked to produce a large facsimile on card with a
translation and explanatory notes. Another group could be asked to
compile the class' growing knowledge of epigraphic conventions and
abbreviations.

2   Work on inscriptions may be extended by a visit to a museum. Pupils should be encouraged to make a careful copy of an inscription and then with appropriate help set about deciphering it. Discourage them from attempting to work on badly damaged or fragmentary inscriptions.

There is unfortunately no simple guide to Roman epigraphy for pupils. Teachers, however, will find a helpful list of formulae in Collingwood and Richmond, Ch.XI; Webster, *A Short Guide to the Roman Inscriptions*.

The Language Information pamphlet

About the language

Nouns (pp. 4–6). The 4th and 5th declensions are now added on p. 6. Pupils have already seen examples of the nominative and accusative in the text but the paradigms are now set out for the first time.

If pupils are dismayed by the appearance of two more noun types point out that the 4th declension embraces a relatively small number of words and the 5th declension even fewer, and that the 5th declension completes the set.

Some pupils may find it helpful to have their attention drawn to
1 the presence of a common vowel, 'u' in the 4th declension, and 'e' in the 5th declension, in many of the cases;
2 similarities between some cases of the 4th and the 2nd declensions (e.g. *manum* and *servum*) and between the 4th and the 3rd declensions (e.g. *manibus* and *cīvibus*).

Note the omission of the ablative as yet from the paradigms. The ablative case by itself, without a preposition, is not introduced until Stage 28, where it is discussed in a language note. It will appear in the tables in the Language Information pamphlet of Unit IIIB.

The exercises in paragraphs 2 and 3 may be supplemented by, for example:

(change from singular to plural)   *dominus amīcō cibum praebuit.*

cubiculum servī prope culīnam erat.

captīvus manum ad custōdēs extendit.

(change from plural to singular)   *pater iuvenibus effigiem dēmōnstrāvit.*

mercātor nōmina nautārum recitāvit.

Adjectives (p. 7). The exercise in paragraph 3 should be led by the teacher and done orally, writing pupils' suggestions on the board. It can be extended by asking pupils to express the noun as well as the adjective in Latin; or the teacher can write up the noun in Latin and ask the class to supply the adjective in agreement with it, using the tables on pp. 4–6.

Further examples:
1 The visitors admired the *beautiful* city.
2 The *huge* lions ran into the arena.
3 The magistrates praised the *good* merchants for their honesty.

4 The commander gave medals to the *brave* slaves.

In three of these the noun and adjective are of different declensions, reinforcing the point that agreement does not necessarily mean identity of ending.

Comparison of adjectives (pp. 8–9). The sentences in paragraph 4 might be continued with more examples, perhaps mixed, to reinforce pupils' awareness of both ways of translating the superlative.

Pronouns (pp. 10–13). Paragraphs 2 and 7: *sē* and *ipse*. The contrast in their usage is not a problem when reading Latin, only when translating into it. The difference may be illustrated by putting pairs of sentences on the board, e.g.

1a *Salvius ipse praemium Belimicō dedit.*

1b *captīvus perterritus sē necāvit.*

2a *prīncipēs sē Salviō trādidērunt.*

2b *custōdēs ipsī captīvōs necāvērunt.*

3a *Quīntus 'pestis, furcifer, asine', sibi inquit.*

3b *Belimicus Agricolae ipsī multa ac falsa nūntiāvit.*

Paragraph 6: in this exercise the class may be asked to translate the noun as well as the demonstrative in sentences 1–5.

Paragraph 8: the relative pronoun. *cuius* and *cui* are now added to the paradigm. The sentences practise identifying the relative clause, the relative pronoun and its antecedent. This may be done orally. The pattern contained in sentences 5 and 6, where the relative pronoun refers to an accusative noun without any expressed subject of the main clause, may cause difficulty. Examples in Unit IIIA include:

> *fibulam, quam puella alia tibi dederat, Vilbiae trādidī.* (Stage 22, p. 30)
>
> *Vilbiam meam, quam valdē amō, auferre audēs?* (Stage 22, p. 36)
>
> *omnēs mīlitēs, quī Dumnorigem custōdīverant, poenās dare iussit.* (Stage 24, p. 65)
>
> *amīcōs igitur, quibus maximē cōnfīdēbat, ad sē vocāvit.* (Stage 28, p. 134)
>
> *ventrem, quī . . . dolēbat, prēnsāvit.* (Stage 28, p. 140)

Paragraph 9: the connecting relative. This should not be tackled until late in the Unit as pupils do not meet it until Stage 27. They often find it awkward at first. It is better not to revise this usage at the same time as other uses of the relative.

Verbs (pp. 14–17). Paragraph 2: it is normally better to conduct this exercise orally. Encourage pupils to detect the clues to the conjugation and show them how to use the 'Words and phrases' section when help is needed. Extend the exercise with examples as required.

In this and similar transformation exercises, pupils should translate, transform and retranslate each word before moving on to the next; they should not work through the whole list translating, then again transforming, since a main purpose of the exercise is that pupils should closely associate change of form (*trāxērunt/trahunt*) with change of meaning (dragged/drag).

Paragraph 7: this exercise while ostensibly about the morphology of the subjunctive gives useful incidental practice in a range of constructions encountered between Stages 24 and 27. It should not be attempted until late in the Unit, by which time the question 'Why is it subjunctive?' can usefully be put to pupils.

Irregular verbs (pp. 18–19). Paragraph 2: further oral practice can be given on these lines.

Paragraph 3: the conjugation of *capiō* causes no problems in reading Latin. Comparison with the imperfect tense of *audiō* and with the present tense of *trahō* will make the point about the 'double category' of this verb, its compounds and a few others such as *faciō*, *rapiō* and *cupiō*.

Uses of the participle (pp. 20–1). Paragraph 4: pupils sometimes confuse the object of a transitive participle with the noun that the participle 'describes'. If they have already translated the participle correctly, in relation to its subject and its object, the solution probably lies in rephrasing the question and asking 'Which noun does the participle agree with?', then doing some further work on the rules of agreement between adjectives and participles and their associated nouns as set out in the next paragraph.

Paragraph 5: when these examples have been translated ask pupils to classify the participle in terms of present or perfect active or perfect passive. This can be extended orally by asking pupils, for instance, to identify the case, number and (where straightforward) gender of participles on this page and in the stages.

Paragraph 7: the perfect participles given here may be varied with other examples and illustrated with an appropriate phrase, such as

nūntius ad rēgem ductus
nūntius ā castrīs profectus

Sometimes a pupil will ask: 'If *parātus* means only "having *been* prepared", how did the Romans say things like "having prepared the dinner, the cook went to sleep"?' Such questions will allow teachers to do some useful preparation for the introduction of the ablative absolute in Stage 31, by saying: 'The Romans had various ways of putting sentences of that kind. One way was to say "with the dinner having been prepared, the cook went to sleep". You will meet examples of this kind in Stage 31.' That should suffice as a trailer. Further analysis at this point is not recommended.

Uses of the subjunctive (pp. 22–4). Paragraph 3: encourage variety of translation of the purpose clause.

Paragraph 6: encourage pupil comment on the two illustrative sentences. The more they try to say about the idea of purpose in the one and the idea of result in the other, the more they will be assessing the meaning of the sentence as a whole, which is the only satisfactory way to comprehend such clauses.

Paragraph 7: indirect command is sometimes confused with purpose clauses. This is not a major cause for concern; their meanings are adjacent and experience will produce more accurate discrimination.

Word order (p. 25). Teachers may wish to give pupils more practice in the deviations from 'normal' word order (nominative + accusative + verb). Two of the commonest are: verb + nominative + accusative (practised here) and accusative + nominative + verb (practised in Unit IIB Language Information pamphlet, p. 19).

While studying paragraph 5 invite comments from the class. It might be left with advantage until Stage 28 and there be used together with the language note on prepositions. The note will enable pupils to express their comments in terms of 'adjective + preposition + noun' or 'preposition + adjective + noun'.

Longer sentences (pp. 26–7). This section provides practice in the more complex sentence patterns developed in Unit IIIA. Three types are represented and the teacher may wish to be aware of them. If a type causes difficulty, more examples should be made up. The types are:

1 'branching' of one participial phrase or subordinate clause out of another; examples are 1c, 4c, 7 and 10;
2 'nesting' of one participial phrase or subordinate clause inside another; examples are 2c, 5c, 8 and 11;
3 'stringing' of two participial phrases or two subordinate clauses, each grammatically related to and dependent on the main clause but not to each other; examples are 3c, 6c, 9 and 12.

Pupils have met 'branching' and 'nesting' of subordinate clauses from Stage 18 and 'stringing' from Stage 20; in Unit IIIA all three types have included participial phrases as well as subordinate clauses. It is unnecessary to present this classification to pupils at this point, although at a later stage some might gain helpful insight by considering it. All that is required here is that pupils should be able to cope practically with these more elaborate sentences. If they get into difficulty in paragraph 3, take them back to shorter versions of the sentence that is causing trouble. For example, sentence 8 can be built up as

8a *lībertus cubiculum intrāre nōlēbat.*

8b *lībertus cubiculum intrāre nōlēbat, quod Memor graviter iam*
   dormiēbat.

Pupils should also be encouraged to read through the longer sentences more than once before trying to translate them.

Words and phrases

Paragraph 3: Ask pupils to translate orally the principal parts into English. This exercise can be extended by giving pupils the principal parts of other familiar verbs for translation.

Linguistic synopsis of Unit IIIA

For general comments, see Unit I Handbook p. 84. LI = Language
Information pamphlet.

Stage	Linguistic feature	Place of language note etc.
21	perfect passive participle (nominative met from Stage 13, accusative from Stage 18)	21, LI
	prepositional phrase and participle (e.g. *ā lībertō excitātus*)	21, LI
	partitive genitive	21
	descriptive genitive	22
	neuter plural	23
	VERB + ACCUSATIVE + NOMINATIVE word order	LI
	DATIVE + VERB + NOMINATIVE word order	
	iubeō/volō + infinitive	
22	perfect active participle (nominative)	22, LI
	descriptive genitive (from Stage 21)	22
	clauses with *cui*	LI
	increasingly varied position of dative	
23	neuter plural (from Stage 21)	23, LI
	genū	LI
	VERB + NOMINATIVE + ACCUSATIVE word order	LI
	īdem	
24	*cum*-clauses	24, LI
	3rd person singular and plural pluperfect subjunctive	24, LI
	3rd person singular and plural imperfect subjunctive (inc. *possum*)	24, LI
	neuter gerundive of obligation	26
	ADJECTIVE + PREPOSITION + NOUN word order	LI

Stage	Linguistic feature	Place of language note etc.
25	indirect question	25, LI
	1st and 2nd persons singular and plural, imperfect and pluperfect subjunctive	25, LI
	perfect active participle (accusative)	LI
	clauses with *cuius*	LI
	dative participle	
	variation of word order in sentences containing infinitive	
26	purpose clause	26, LI
	neuter gerundive of obligation (from Stage 24)	26
	impersonal verbs	27
	expressions of time	28
	num + indirect question	LI
	more complex examples of 'stringing' and 'nesting' (see p. 74 above)	LI
	id quod, ea quae	
	dative + participle (e.g. *hīs verbīs diffīsus*)	
27	indirect command	27, LI
	result clause	27, LI
	impersonal verbs (from Stage 26)	27
	extended prepositional phrase + participle (e.g. *ē manibus Britannōrum ēlāpsus*)	
	DATIVE + NOMINATIVE + ACCUSATIVE + VERB word order	
28	ablative	28
	ablative + participle (e.g. *morbō afflīctus*)	28
	expressions of time (from Stage 26)	28
	prepositions	28
	connecting relative (one in Stage 26)	LI
	more complex examples of 'branching' (see p. 74 above)	LI
	more complex *cui*-clauses; *quibus*-clauses	

The following terms are used in Unit IIIA. Numerals indicate the stage in which each is introduced.

perfect passive participle	21	impersonal	27
perfect active participle	22	result clause	27
subjunctive	24	ablative	28
direct and indirect question	25	preposition	28
purpose clause	26	comparison	LI
gerundive	26	connecting relative	LI
direct and indirect command	27	indicative	LI

Appendix A: Attainment tests

For notes on the purpose of the attainment tests, and suggestions for their use, see Unit I Handbook, p. 88. The words in heavy print have not occurred in the stage checklists. A few words not in the checklists are not in heavy print, if their meaning is obvious or if they have been prominent in the preceding stage.

Test 7

This test should be worked after the class has finished Stage 22. The story should be given to pupils in three separate parts, preferably in three consecutive periods.

Part I: introduction

This should be translated orally and informally with the class, so that the pupils become familiar with the situation and context of the story. This will probably not take more than fifteen minutes at the end of a lesson.

amōrēs Modestī
Modestus, ubi Aquās Sūlis vīsitābat, multās puellās **adamāvit**, sed celeriter **dēseruit**. Scapha, fīlia mercātōris, prīma eum dēlectāvit. Modestus eī rosās dedit quās ex hortō Memoris **abstulerat**.
    'volō tē hoc dōnum accipere', inquit, 'quod puellam pulchriōrem quam tē numquam vīdī. sine tē vīvere nōn possum.'   5
    'ō Modeste', respondit Scapha **ērubēscēns**, 'ego quoque tē **cōnspicāta**, statim adamāvī. volō dōnum parvum tibi dare, quod vir magnae **benignitātis** es.'
    ubi haec verba dīxit, gemmam pretiōsam Modestō dedit.

Part II: written translation

After a brief oral recapitulation of Part I, the pupils should be asked to translate Part II. We suggest a whole period should be allowed for this written translation.

postrīdiē Ampelīsca, **ōrnātrīx** perīta, ad fontem sacrum   10
prōcēdēbat. Modestus, eam **secūtus**, post columnam sē cēlāvit.
Ampelīsca, deam precāta, postquam nōnnūllōs **sēstertiōs** in aquam

iniēcit, ā fonte sacrō abībat. Modestus eī obstitit.

'ego tē nōn nōvī', inquit, 'sed volō tē hoc dōnum accipere, quod
puellam pulchriōrem quam tē numquam vīdī. sine tē vīvere nōn   15
possum.'

haec verba locūtus, gemmam, quam ā Scaphā accēperat, eī
dedit. Ampelīsca, maximē attonita, **prīmō** dōnum accipere
nōlēbat, sed, ā Modestō **identidem** rogāta, cōnsēnsit.

tum Modestus 'necesse est nōbīs', inquit, 'iterum convenīre.   20
multa alia dōna dare tibi volō.'

'ō Modeste!' exclāmāvit Ampelīsca, 'quam līberālis es! ego
quoque tibi aliquid dare volō.'

et ānulum aureum, quem in **digitō** habēbat, eī trādidit.

Part III: comprehension test

The passage and the comprehension questions should be given to pupils
in the next Latin lesson. A mark-scheme has been suggested but teachers
may wish to award marks differently.

post paucōs diēs, Modestus ē thermīs **ēgressus**, aliam puellam   25
prope templum stantem cōnspexit. ubi eī appropinquāvit,

'hercle', inquit, 'nōnne tū es dea Minerva ipsa?'

'minimē', respondit puella, 'ego sum Scintilla.'

'et quid in hōc oppidō agis, Scintilla?' rogāvit Modestus.

'**ostreās** in forō vēndō', respondit Scintilla.   30

'quam fēlīcēs sunt illae ostreae', inquit Modestus, 'quod manūs
tuae eās **tangunt**.'

tum ānulum aureum, quem ab Ampelīscā accēperat, Scintillae
dedit.

'volō tē hoc dōnum accipere', inquit, 'quod puellam   35
pulchriōrem quam tē numquam vīdī. sine tē nōn vīvere possum.'

Scintilla ānulum acceptum intentē spectāvit. subitō Modestum
vehementer verberāre coepit.

'parce! parce!' clāmāvit Modestus. 'cūr tū, cui ānulum dedī, mē
pulsās?'   40

Scintilla īrāta respondit, 'tē pulsō, quod ānulum agnōscō.
Ampelīsca, soror mea, mīlitī Rōmānō, quī amōrem **aeternum**
prōmīsit, hunc ānulum dedit. tū es mīles iste. Ampelīsca, ā tē
dēcepta, trīstissima est. nunc igitur tē pūniō.'

Modestus, ā Scintillā ita verberātus, quam celerrimē effūgit.   45

Marks

1   Where had Modestus been? Where did he see the girl?   2

2   'nōnne tū es dea Minerva ipsa?' (line 27). Why do you think
     that Modestus said this to the girl?   2
3   What did the girl tell Modestus about herself?   2
4   Why did Modestus say the oysters were fortunate?   2
5   What present did Modestus give to the girl? How had he
     come by it?   2
6   Why was Modestus surprised by the girl's reaction?   2
7   Why did the girl recognise the present?   2
8   Why was Ampelisca 'trīstissima' (line 44)?   2
9   What is the last thing we hear about Modestus in this story? 2
10 Having read all three parts of the story, what have you
     learnt about Modestus' character?   2
                                                                    _____
                                                                        20

Teachers may like to note how pupils are coping with the following
features in particular:

neuter plurals: *haec verba* (line 9); *multa alia dōna* (21).
participial phrases: (i) perfect passive: *Ampelīsca ... ā Modestō identidem
  rogāta* (18–19); *Ampelīsca, ā tē dēcepta* (43–4); (ii) perfect active: *Ampelīsca,
  deam precāta* (12); *haec verba locūtus* (17).
volō: with accusative and present infinitive *volō tē ... accipere* (4 and 14), as
  contrasted with examples with present infinitive alone *volō ... dare* (7);
  ego ... dare volō (22–3).
relative clauses containing oblique cases of the relative pronoun: *quās ...
  abstulerat* (3); *quam ... accēperat* (17); *quem ... habēbat* (24); *quem ...
  accēperat* (33); *cui ānulum dedī* (39).
complex sentences: *Ampelīsca ... abībat* (12–13); *haec ... dedit* (17–18);
  Ampelīsca ... cōnsēnsit (18–19).
position of dative: the test contains many examples of the dative
  (particularly *eī*) in a variety of positions within the sentence; check that
  pupils can recognise their forms and functions.

Test 8

This test should be worked after the class has finished Stage 26. It is
suggested that the same procedure should be followed as for Test 7.

Part I: introduction: for oral translation

Agricola Calēdoniōs vincit
Agricola, cum Britanniam quīnque annōs administrāvisset, **contrā**
Calēdoniōs bellum gerere **cōnstituit**. nāvēs igitur ēmīsit ut portūs

barbarōrum explōrārent. ipse **simul** in Calēdoniam cum magnīs
cōpiīs prōcessit.

Calēdoniī, ubi nāvēs Rōmānōrum vīdērunt, valdē commōtī, sē   5
ad bellum parāvērunt.

Agricola, cum barbarīs appropinquāret, cōpiās suās in trēs
partēs **dīvīsit**. barbarī, hoc cōnspicātī, in **nōnam** legiōnem, quae
erat pars **invalidissima**, **noctū** impetum facere cōnstituērunt.
castra ingressī, cum custōdēs interfēcissent, mīlitēs dormientēs   10
oppugnāvērunt. Agricola, postquam ab **explōrātōribus** cognōvit
quid accidisset, ad castra cum novīs cōpiīs statim contendit. pugna
erat **ātrōx**. tandem barbarī, magnā cum difficultāte superātī, in
silvās et **palūdēs** effūgērunt.

Part II: written translation

Before this is undertaken it will be helpful to revise the military
vocabulary of Part I and to make sure everyone is clear about the story so
far.

post illam pugnam Rōmānī in ultimās partēs Calēdoniae   15
contendēbant. Calēdoniī, cum uxōrēs **līberōs**que in loca tūta
dūxissent, magnās **cōpiās** collēgērunt. ad montem Graupium
prōgressī, sē ad pugnam parāvērunt. tum Calgācus, prīnceps
Calēdoniōrum, quī erat vir summae virtūtis, haec verba dīxit:

'ō Calēdoniī, hodiē nōs prō **lībertāte patriae** pugnāmus; nam   20
istī Rōmānī omnēs aliōs Britannōs iam superāvērunt. Rōmānī, quī
numquam contentī sunt, omnēs hominēs vincere cupiunt; ad
omnēs partēs **orbis terrārum** legiōnēs dūcunt; ab omnibus
gentibus pecūniam **opēs**que rapiunt; fēminās līberōsque in
servitūtem trahunt. necesse est **aut** Rōmānōs **expellere aut** prō   25
lībertāte pugnantēs perīre.'

Part III: comprehension test

Calēdoniī, cum verba Calgācī audīvissent, vehementer plausērunt
et magnō cum clāmōre pugnam poposcērunt.

Agricola, quamquam Rōmānī quoque pugnāre valdē cupiēbant,
pauca dīcere **cōnstituit**:   30

'vōs, mīlitēs Rōmānī, multōs labōrēs passī, tandem in ultimās
partēs Calēdoniae pervēnistis. vōs saepe, cum per silvās, per
flūmina, per montēs mēcum iter facerētis, **fīnem** labōrum vidēre
nōn poterātis. saepe **dubitābātis** num dī Rōmānīs favērent. hodiē

tamen tōta Britannia est nostra. vincite et barbarōs in mare   35
pellite.'

haec locūtus Agricola mīlitēs impetum facere iussit. Rōmānī
fortiter pugnābant, sed hostēs ferōciter resistēbant. multī
utrimque periērunt. Agricola ipse ex equō dēscendit ut **ante**
vexilla cum mīlitibus stāret. Rōmānī, cum hoc vīdissent, hostēs   40
fortissimē oppugnāvērunt et fugere coēgērunt. tum equitēs, ab
Agricolā iussī, multōs barbarōs fugientēs interfēcērunt. paucī ex
illā pugnā superfuērunt; **aliī** domōs suās incendērunt; **aliī** uxōrēs
līberōsque necāvērunt, quod nōlēbant eōs esse servōs
Rōmānōrum. postrīdiē Rōmānī nūllōs barbarōs invenīre poterant   45
nisi mortuōs.

1	How did the Caledonii react to Calgacus' speech?	2
2	What were the feelings of the Roman troops before Agricola spoke to them (lines 29–30)?	1
3	Why had the Romans' march north been so difficult?	2
4	According to Agricola, what doubt had his men had about the gods (line 34)?	1
5	What did Agricola urge his men to do in the last sentence of his speech?	2
6	Which side attacked first? Give one reason for your answer.	2
7	What did Agricola do in the battle to encourage his men (lines 39–40)?	2
8	What was the result of his encouragement?	2
9	What job did Agricola give to the horsemen at the end of the battle?	1
10	What did the Caledonian survivors do after the battle (lines 43–4)?	2
11	'necāvērunt' (line 44): why did they do this?	1
12	Which word is given special emphasis in the last sentence? Why is this?	2

20

Pupils may find the military content and the rhetorical style of the
speeches in this passage more demanding than the straightforward
narrative and dialogue of previous tests. Teachers may like to assess
whether the pupils' grasp of morphology, syntax and basic vocabulary is
firm enough to help them overcome any problems presented by less
familiar subject matter. The following features have been recently
introduced in the Course:

adjective + preposition + noun word order: *magnā cum difficultāte* (13);
magnō cum clāmōre (28).
cum with imperfect subjunctive: *cum ... appropinquāret* (7).
cum with pluperfect subjunctive: *cum ... interfēcissent* (10); *cum ... dūxissent*
(16–17).
indirect question: *Agricola ... accidisset* (11–12); *saepe ... favērent* (34).
purpose clause: *nāvēs ... explōrārent* (2–3); *Agricola ... stāret* (39–40).
Teachers may also like to check on pupils' ability to handle the numerous
participial phrases in the passage and analyse whether they can
distinguish correctly between the different cases, tenses and voices of the
participles.

Test 9

This test should be worked after the class has finished Stage 28. It is
suggested that the same procedure should be followed as for Test 7.

Part I: introduction: for oral translation

Modestus aegrōtat

ōlim Modestus et Strȳthiō cēnābant. cibus tamen quem coquus
parāverat pessimus erat. subitō Modestus, coquum vehementer
dētestātus, cibum humī dēiēcit.

'iste coquus', inquit, 'est **venēficus**. cibum pessimum nōbīs
semper parat.'   5

'cibum meliōrem comparāre nōn possumus', inquit Strȳthiō. 'nam
nūllam pecūniam habēmus. melius est perīre quam miserē vīvere.'

Modestus, homō summae calliditātis, cum haec verba audīvisset,
cōnsilium cēpit. Strȳthiōnem iussit amīcōs quaerere et haec nūntiāre,

'Modestus, amīcus noster cārissimus, graviter **aegrōtat**. cum eum   10
vīsitārem tam sollicitus erat ut dē testāmentō cōgitāret. ille tamen,
quamquam gravī morbō **afflīctus**, maximē **sitit** et **ēsurit**. nōs igitur
oportet eī cibum vīnumque ferre.'

Part II: written translation

Strȳthiō, ā Modestō missus, amīcōs quaesīvit ut verba Modestī eīs
nūntiāret. cum Aulum et Pūblicum et Nigrīnam invēnisset tōtam   15
rem nārrāvit.

Aulus, hīs verbīs dēceptus, sibi dīxit,

'volō Modestum mihi aliquid **lēgāre**. mihi necesse est Modestō
dōnum splendidum dare.'

itaque Aulus, amphoram vīnī optimī adeptus, ad cubiculum   20

Modestī laetus contendit. Nigrīna et Pūblicus tamen trīstissimī erant.
Nigrīna Modestō magnum **piscem** coquere cōnstituit. Pūblicus ad
forum cucurrit ut **pānem** et **ōva** comparāret.

amīcī, ubi cubiculō, in quō Modestus iacēbat, appropinquābant,
gemitūs lacrimāsque audīvērunt. Strȳthiō, ē cubiculō ēgressus,   25
'morbus Modestī **ingravēscit**', inquit. 'vōbīs melius est mihi
dōna dare et discēdere.'

cum amīcī discessissent sollicitī, Modestus et Strȳthiō rīdentēs
magnificē cēnāvērunt. post cēnam Modestus tam **ēbrius** erat ut
multās hōrās dormīret.   30

postrīdiē amīcī ad cubiculum rediērunt, ut cognōscerent quid
accidisset. Strȳthiō, **reditūs** amīcōrum ignārus, per castra
ambulābat. amīcī, in cubiculum ingressī, circumspectāvērunt.
Modestum immōtum in lectō iacentem vīdērunt.

Part III: comprehension test

'ēheu! mortuus est Modestus', inquit Nigrīna. lacrimīs sē dedit.   35
Aulus, nihil locūtus, testāmentum Modestī quaerēbat.

'amīcum fortissimum āmīsimus', inquit Pūblicus. 'nōbīs
decōrum est eum magnō cum honōre **sepelīre**.'

Pūblicus statim ēgressus **libitīnāriō** imperāvit ut ad cubiculum
festīnāret. **brevī** tempore advēnērunt libitīnārius et quattuor servī,   40
arcam ferentēs. tam gravis erat Modestus ut difficile esset servīs
eum in arcam pōnere.

tandem servī Modestum in arcā positum magnā cum difficultāte
in umerōs sustulērunt. libitīnārius ē cubiculō prīmus prōcēdēbat,
post eum amīcī; servī, ultimī ēgressī, arcam ferēbant.   45

Strȳthiō, ad cubiculum tandem regressus, in libitīnārium
violenter incurrit. quī attonitus in servōs incidit. servī arcam tenēre
nōn poterant. magnō cum **fragōre** humī dēcidit arca. magnus
clāmor erat. omnēs Strȳthiōnem vituperābant.

subitō vōcem **raucam** audīvērunt: 'nōlīte clāmāre.'   50

amīcī, cum tacitī **respexissent**, Modestum ex arcā surgentem
vīdērunt.

'umbra est Modestī', inquit Nigrīna perterrita. 'nōbīs fugiendum
est.'

fūgērunt aliī omnēs. Strȳthiō tamen adeō attonitus erat ut fugere   55
nōn posset. Modestum sollicitus rogāvit num mortuus esset.

'minimē', respondit Modestus. 'morbum, nōn mortem **simulāvī**.
nunc tamen mihi nōn necesse est morbum simulāre; quod nimium
vīnī cōnsūmpsī, **rē vērā** aegrōtō.'

1 'mortuus est Modestus' (line 35). What do you think were the feelings of the three friends at this news? Give reasons for your answer. 3

2 How did the 'libitīnārius' come to appear on the scene? 1

3 Whom did he bring with him? 1

4 What was their job? Why did they find it difficult on this occasion? 2

5 'magnō cum fragōre humī dēcidit arca' (line 48). First translate this sentence, and then explain in your own words what sequence of events had led to this happening. 2+3

6 To whom did the 'vōx rauca' (line 50) belong? 1

7 What was he doing? 1

8 Which Latin word tells you that he was obeyed? 1

9 What did Nigrina think she was seeing? 1

10 What did she and her friends then do? 1

11 Why did Strythio not do the same thing? 1

12 In line 56 who asked the question? 1

13 From the last sentence do you conclude that the speaker is now

(a) dead   (d) ill

(b) pretending to be dead   (e) pretending to be ill?

(c) pretending to be well 1

20

Teachers may like to note how pupils are coping with the following features in particular:

vocabulary: most of the vocabulary in this passage should be familiar and several 'obvious' words have not been glossed although they have not occurred in the checklists so far. See whether the pupils can connect *miserē* (7) with the familiar *miser*; *calliditās* (8) with *callidus*; *regressus* (46) with *ēgressus, ingressus*; *incurrit* (47) with *currō*.

extended participial phrases: *amphoram vīnī optimī adeptus* (20); *reditūs amīcōrum ignārus* (32).

participial phrases containing ablatives: *gravī morbō afflīctus* (12); *hīs verbīs dēceptus* (17).

result clauses: *cum ... cōgitāret* (10–11); *post cēnam ... dormīret* (29–30); *tam gravis ... pōnere* (41–2); *Strȳthiō ... nōn posset* (55–6).

indirect question: *postrīdiē ... accidisset* (31–2).

connecting relative: *quī ... incidit* (47).

'nesting': *amīcī ... audīvērunt* (24–5).

'branching': *postrīdiē ... accidisset* (31–2).

Appendix B: Words and phrases in Unit IIIA checklists

The numeral indicates the stage in which the word or phrase appears in a checklist

ā (= 'by') (21)
ac (28)
accidere (25)
accūsāre (26)
adeō (27)
adipīscī (22)
aditus (27)
adiuvāre (21)
administrāre (23)
adstāre (24)
adventus (27)
aliquis (25)
amor (22)
annus (21)
anteā (27)
aperīre (25)
appārēre (27)
ardēre (27)
arrogantia (28)
ascendere (21)
atque (28)
auctōritās (24)
audāx (24)
auferre (26)
aureus (22)
autem (25)
avidē (22)

barbarus (21)
bellum (26)
bellum gerere (26)
beneficium (28)

caelum (22)

captīvus (25)
carcer (24)
castra (25)
cēdere (23)
cēlāre (21)
centum (28)
certāmen (27)
circum (21)
clārus (23)
cōgere (25)
cohors (26)
colligere (26)
colloquium (24)
comes (27)
commemorāre (23)
commōtus (26)
comprehendere (24)
cōnfīdere (21)
cōnscendere (24)
cōnspicārī (23)
cōnstituere (28)
corpus (28)
cum (= 'when') (24)
cūra (23)

decem (20 + 28)
decēre (27)
dēcipere (22)
dēicere (21)
dēpōnere (25)
dēscendere (24)
dēserere (24)
dēsinere (25)
dī immortālēs (25)

dignitās (25)
dīligentia (25)
dīligere (28)
dīrus (22)
dissentīre (22)
docēre (26)
dolēre (28)
ducentī (28)
duo (12, 20 + 28)
dūrus (21)

efficere (21)
ēgredī (24)
ēligere (22)
enim (23)
eques (24)
errāre (23)
exitium (22)
explicāre (25)
extrā (25)
extrahere (21)

facinus (26)
falsus (26)
fax (27)
fidēs (26)
flūmen (24)
fōns (21)
fundere (22)
furēns (25)

gaudēre (27)
gemitus (28)
gerere (23)

gravis (21)

haesitāre (25)
haruspex (21)
hērēs (28)
honor (23)
hōra (21)
hostis (22)
humī (24)

iacere (23)
iactāre (22)
ignārus (27)
immemor (25)
immortālis (25)
immōtus (23)
imperāre (27)
incendere (27)
incipere (22)
induere (23)
īnfēlīx (21)
īnfestus (24)
ingenium (23)
ingredī (22)
inicere (22)
īnsānus (26)
īnsidiae (27)
īnstruere (26)
intereā (24)
iocus (27)
īra (28)
iubēre (21)
iussum (27)

lacrima (22)
laedere (25)
latēre (25)
lēgātus (26)
legiō (25)
lingua (28)
loquī (23)

magnopere (24)

malus (28)
mandāre (28)
mandātum (23)
manus (= 'band') (27)
maximē (24)
metus (28)
mīlia (28)
mīlle (28)
minimus (22)
modus (23)
molestus (22)
monēre (22)
morbus (21)
multō (28)

neque ... neque (24)
nescīre (25)
nimium (23)
nocēre (27)
nōmen (25)
nōnāgintā (28)
nōnnūllī (21)
novem (20 + 28)
num' (26)
numerus (23)
nūper (21)
nusquam (24)

occīdere (28)
occupāre (26)
occupātus (21)
occurrere (27)
octō (20 + 28)
octōgintā (28)
opēs (28)
oportet (26)
oppidum (21)
oppugnāre (24)
ōrnāre (23)
ōs (= 'face') (25)
ōsculum (27)

pallidus (28)

parcere (22)
pārēre (23)
patefacere (24)
patī (24)
perfidia (26)
perfidus (24)
perītus (21)
plēnus (21)
plūs (21)
poena (25)
poenās dare (25)
pōns (24)
potēns (23)
praebēre (26)
praeceps (27)
praeficere (28)
praemium (27)
prāvus (23)
precārī (22)
pretium (21)
prīncipia (26)
prōvincia (26)
proximus (27)
prūdentia (22)

quadrāgintā (20 + 28)
quālis (27)
quantus (22)
quattuor (20 + 28)
quicquam (28)
quīnquāgintā (20 + 28)
quīnque (20 + 28)
quō modō? (22)
quot (26)

referre (26)
rēgnum (26)
regredī (23)
rīpa (24)
rursus (25)

saevus (26)
sānē (26)

sapiēns (21)
scelestus (25)
scīre (23)
septem (20 + 28)
septuāgintā (28)
sex (20 + 28)
sexāgintā (28)
sī (26)
sīc (28)
silentium (27)
solvere (28)
spēs (28)
statiō (25)
suāvis (25)
sub (27)
suscipere (21)

suspicārī (28)

tacitus (27)
taedēre (27)
tālis (23)
tamquam (23)
tantum (24)
tantus (27)
tardus (22)
testāmentum (28)
testis (25)
trānsīre (24)
trēs (12, 20 + 28)
tribūnus (26)
trīgintā (20 + 28)
trīstis (24)
tūtus (22)

ultimus (26)
umquam (23)
unde (21)
ūnus (12, 20 + 28)
ut (= 'as') (28)
ut (= 'that') (26)

venēnum (23)
venia (23)
ventus (28)
verbum (22)
vērum (24)
vīgintī (20 + 28)
virtūs (22)
vītāre (22)

Appendix C: Summary of changes from the first edition of the course

Changes in Unit IIIA include the following:

1 The original Stages 21–25 have been reorganised into new Stages 21–28.

2 The length of the **reading material** has been reduced by about 135 lines and the new **vocabulary** by about 70 words. Some stories have been subdivided.

3 The perfect passive participle is now introduced and explained separately from the perfect active participle. It is also rehearsed more intensively in the reading material. The introduction of the ablative case has been simplified: the number of usages has been restricted, each usage is described explicitly and the number of examples of each usage has been greatly increased.

4 New **model sentences** have been written for new Stages 21, 22, 25, 27 and 28.

5 New **language notes** include comment on the perfect participle, subjunctive usages and the ablative case.

6 Many new **manipulation exercises** have been added and most of the original ones, especially those that were purely translation, have been omitted.

7 Many more **illustrations** have been provided.

8 New **background material** deals with Roman religion, travel and communication, Agricola and the sources of our knowledge of Roman Britain.

9 New **attainment tests** have been added to follow new Stages 22 and 26.

Bibliography

Books

This list has necessarily to be selective but is also intended to extend that in the Teacher's Handbook to Unit IIA (pp. 43–6). Books marked * are suitable for pupils. Some of the others would also be suitable for pupils to refer to under the teacher's guidance. Some recommended out-of-print (O.P.) books are included in case teachers already possess them or can obtain second-hand copies.

General

Balsdon, J. P. V. D. *Life and Leisure in Ancient Rome* (Bodley Head 1969)

Birley, A. R. *Life in Roman Britain* (Batsford, rev. edn 1976)

Branigan, K. *Roman Britain: Life in an Imperial Province* (Life in Britain Series: Reader's Digest 1980)

Cambridge School Classics Project *The Romans Discover Britain* and *Teacher's Handbook* (C.U.P. 1981)

  The Roman World Units I and II (C.U.P. 1978–9) and *Teacher's Handbook* (C.U.P. 1980)

Carcopino, J. *Daily Life in Ancient Rome* (Routledge 1973 O.P.; Penguin 1970)

Casson, L. *Ships and Seamanship in the Ancient World* (Princeton U.P. 1971) *Travel in the Ancient World* (Allen and Unwin 1974)

Chevallier, R. *Roman Roads* (Batsford 1976)

Collingwood, R. G. and Richmond I. A. *The Archaeology of Roman Britain* (Methuen, rev. edn 1969)

Cunliffe, B. *Rome and her Empire* (Bodley Head 1978)

Dudley, D. R. *Urbs Roma* (Phaidon 1967 O.P.)

Ferguson, J. *Religions of the Roman Empire* (Thames and Hudson 1970 O.P.; pbk 1982)

Frere, S. S. and St Joseph, J. K. *Roman Britain from the Air* (C.U.P. 1983)

Hattatt, R. *Ancient and Romano-British Brooches* (Dorset Publishing Company 1982)

Margary, I. D. *Roman Roads in Britain* (Baker, 3rd edn 1973)

Ogilvie, R. M. *The Romans and their Gods* (Chatto and Windus 1970)

Ordnance Survey *Map of Roman Britain* (H.M.S.O. 1979)

Paoli, U. E. *Rome, its People, Life and Customs* (Longman 1963)

Tacitus *Agricola*; ed. R. M. Ogilvie and I. A. Richmond (Oxford U.P. 1967)

Tacitus *On Britain and Germany*; translated by H. Mattingly (Penguin 1948)

Van der Heyden, A. A. M. and Scullard, H. H. **Atlas of the Classical World* (Nelson 1959 O.P.)

Wacher, J. *The Towns of Roman Britain* (Batsford 1975; pbk 1978)

Aquae Sulis

Cunliffe, B. *Aquae Sulis (History Patch Series (pbk): Ginn 1971)
  Roman Bath (Oxford U.P. 1969 O.P.)
  Roman Bath Discovered (Routledge 1971 O.P.)
  The Roman Baths: a Guide to the Baths and Roman Museum (Bath Archaeological Trust 1978 O.P.)

Hassall, M. 'From our correspondent in Roman Britain: The fountain of Sulis' *Omnibus* I 1981, p. 16
  'Religion in Roman Britain with example of a project kit on the cult of Minerva' *Hesperiam* no. 2 1979, pp. 18–33

Stewart, B. *The Roman Baths and Museum* (Unichrome of Bath 1983)
  **Waters of the Gap: the Mythology of Aquae Sulis* (Bath City Council pbk 1981)

Further information on the latest excavations is available from Bath City Council, Dept of Leisure and Tourist Services, Bath BA1 1LZ.

Deva

Collingwood, R. G. and Wright, R. P. 'The Roman Inscriptions in the Grosvenor Museum, Chester' Reprinted from *R.I.B.* pp. 146–90, with addenda by G. L. Morgan and D. J. Robinson. (Grosvenor Museum Publications 1978)

Grosvenor Museum Education Service *The Deva Investigation Book* (Grosvenor Museum Publications rev. edn 1982 O.P.)

Petch, D. R. *Deva Victrix (History Patch Series (pbk): Ginn 1971)

Strickland, T. J. *Roman Chester* (Grosvenor Museum Publications 1984)

Strickland, T. J. and Davey, P. J. *New Evidence for Roman Chester* (Grosvenor Museum Publications 1978 O.P.)

Webster, G. **A Short Guide to the Roman Inscriptions and Sculptured Stones in the Grosvenor Museum, Chester* (Grosvenor Museum Publications rev. edn 1970 O.P.)

Further information, including quiz sheets and project books for school children and a publications list, is available from the Grosvenor Museum Education Service, 27 Grosvenor Street, Chester CH1 2DD.

See also *J.A.C.T. Bulletin* 63 Autumn 1983 pp. 26–7 for article on the Museum.

The Roman army

All the materials listed in this section could be used by pupils, though guidance will of course be needed.

Abranson, E. *Roman Legionaries at the time of Julius Caesar* (Macdonald 1979)

Birley, R. *Vindolanda: a Roman Frontier Post on Hadrian's Wall* (Thames and Hudson, rev. edn 1979)
Vindolanda in Colour (Frank Graham 1974)

Breeze, D. J. and Dobson, B. *Hadrian's Wall* (Allen Lane 1976; Penguin 1978)

Connolly, P. *The Roman Army* (Macdonald 1975)

Dobson, B. and Breeze, D. J. *The Army of Hadrian's Wall* (Frank Graham 1972 O.P.)

Embleton, R. *Hadrian's Wall Reconstructed* (Frank Graham 1974)

Hodge, P. *The Roman Army* (Aspects of Roman Life Series: Longman 1978)

Jones, D. and Jones, P. *Hadrian's Wall* (Jackdaw Series 41: Cape 1968 O.P.)

Martin, C. 'The Gods of the Imperial Roman Army' *History Today* Vol. 19 April 1969

Pictorial Education Quarterly, Summer 1975: *The Roman Army* (based on P. Connolly's book above) (Evans Bros, Montague House, Russell Square, London WC1B 5BX)

Powell, G. 'The Roman Legions and their Officers' *History Today* Vol. 17 November 1967

Richmond, I. A. 'Trajan's Army on Trajan's Column' *Papers of the British School at Rome* Vol. 13 1935, pp. 1–40

Robinson, H. R. *The Armour of Imperial Rome* (Arms and Armour Press 1975 O.P.)
The Armour of the Roman Legions (Frank Graham 1980 O.P.)
The Roman Army: set of sheets to cut out and colour. Available at many museums and from Iceni Publications, 79 Peace Road, Stanway, Colchester, Essex
What the Soldiers Wore on Hadrian's Wall (Frank Graham 1976 O.P.)

Rossi, L. *Trajan's Column and the Dacian Wars* (Thames and Hudson 1971)

Simkins, M. *The Roman Army from Caesar to Trajan* (Osprey pbk 1974)

Times Newspapers Ltd, Printing House Square, London EC1: *Wallchart The Roman Army* (rev. edn 1972)

Warry, J. *Warfare in the Classical World* (Salamander Books 1970 O.P.)

Watson, G. R. *The Roman Soldier* (Thames and Hudson 1969)

Webster, G. *The Roman Army* (Grosvenor Museum Publications 1956
    O.P.)
    The Roman Imperial Army (A. C. Black, rev. edn 1979)
Wilkes, J. *The Roman Army* (C.U.P. 1972)
Wilson, R. *Roman Forts: An Illustrated Introduction to the Garrison Posts of
    Roman Britain* (Bergström & Boyle Books 1980)

Source material and reference

Ferguson, J. and Chisholm, K. *Rome – the Augustan Age: a Sourcebook*
    (Oxford U.P. 1981)
Lewis, N. and Reinhold, M. *Roman Civilisation: a Sourcebook. I The Republic;
    II The Empire* (Harper Torchbooks: Harper and Row 1966)
London Association of Classical Teachers. Lactor No. 4: *Some Inscriptions
    from Roman Britain* (L.A.C.T. 1969)
    Lactor No. 8: *Inscriptions of the Roman Empire* (L.A.C.T. 1971)
    Both these include translations and are obtainable from Dr J. Roy,
    Dept of Ancient History and Classical Archaeology, The University,
    Sheffield S10 2TN.
R.I.B. – Collingwood, R. G. and Wright, R. P. *The Roman Inscriptions of
    Britain Vol. I: Inscriptions on Stone* (Oxford U.P. 1965)

Slides and filmstrips

In addition to the Cambridge Classical Filmstrip 2, 'Roman Britain', the
following may be found helpful. The materials listed below are only a
selection from the slides and filmstrips available; there is a large amount
that bears on the Roman Army in Britain, and the items included are
mostly among the more recent publications. Suppliers are listed at the
end.

Strips and slides offering a general coverage of Roman Britain were
listed in the Unit IIA Handbook.

Stage 21
White, H. A. B. and H. R. B. *Aquae Sulis*. Double-frame colour filmstrip,
40 frames, with notes; also available as slides. This full and colourful
treatment makes clear the development of the Roman Baths site and its
relationship to the city as a whole. It takes into account excavations up to
the end of 1979. As well as the major finds such as the head of Minerva,
the strip includes a number of smaller objects such as gems, and several
inscriptions. (H. A. B. White; or from Bath Museum, who also publish
some sets of 3 slides)

Stage 23
Sudhalter, R. *et al. Religion in Roman Life*. See Unit IIB Handbook, p. 92.

As it traces the growth of Roman religion and its importance to individual and state, this filmstrip is quite relevant to this stage. (Educational Audio Visual Q2170, cassette included)

Stage 24

Green, A. C. and Forrest, M. St J. *Roman Roads*. Single-frame colour filmstrip with 21 frames of artist's reconstructions, plus optional cassette. Includes a section on transport. (Visual Publications PD3)

Stage 25

Newcastle Museum of Antiquities publishes a substantial list of colour slides relating to the Army, most but not all associated with Hadrian's Wall. Sold singly.

Pictorial Colour Slides: see Unit IIA Handbook, p. 47, for fuller list; the following sets are particularly relevant here:

Hadrian's Wall. 20 colour slides. Includes several granaries, Housesteads principia and latrines, Chesters bath-house, etc. (Set 11)

Models and Reconstructions. 25 colour slides. Includes a number of military items, e.g. ballista, onager, aries, siege-tower, and fortifications. (Set 12)

Inscriptions, Coins and Tile Stamps. 20 colour slides. Has six military tombstones (some are also in the C.L.C. material), legionary tile stamps, lead pig, etc. (Set 15)

Dalladay, R. L. *Soldiers of Trajan* and *Trajan on Campaign*. Two short filmstrips, each double-frame, colour, 12 frames, with notes; or as slides. They illustrate the composition of the Imperial army, and the life of the soldier in camp and in the field, from close-ups of Trajan's Column. (Ministrips C2, C3 from R. L. Dalladay)

Fines, John. *The Roman Army in Britain*. Double- or single-frame colour filmstrip, with notes. A recent strip which uses original monuments and objects, with reconstructions. Sold on its own or in a boxed set with *Towns in Roman Britain* and *Living in Roman Britain*, under the overall title of *The Romans in Britain*. The full set has additional teaching suggestions. (Longman/Common Ground 24161 DF or 2417X SF; boxed set, 22789 DF or 2420X SF)

Green, A. C. and Forrest, M. St J. *Roman Forts and Walls*. Single-frame colour filmstrip, 23 frames, optional cassette, notes; see Unit IIA Handbook, p. 46. (Visual Publications PD4)

Jones, G. D. B. *Hadrian's Wall from the Air*. Set of 16 colour slides, good clear air photos, with substantial notes. (Archaeological Advisers Ltd)

Lishman, E. P. *Roman Britain*. See Unit IIA Handbook, p. 46, for this strip which has a military emphasis. (Focal Point FP180)

Bibliography

Lucas-Dean Films. *The Roman Occupation of Britain: Fortifications* and *The Roman Occupation of Britain: Weapons.* Two double-frame filmstrips, colour, 37 and 18 frames, notes. *Fortifications* includes the general strategy of conquest, with maps; *Weapons* has two useful diagrams of army organisation and diagrams and models of legionary arms and armour, and artillery. Attractively presented and clear on what they cover. (Viewtech)

Smith, D. J. *Roman Britain: Fortifications.* See Unit IIA Handbook, p. 47. (Hugh Baddeley, through Slide Centre HB115)

Zidik, J. and Chase, M. *The Roman Army.* Single-frame colour filmstrip, 35 frames, notes. A traditional strip with mostly black-and-white drawings and photos with some coloured diagrams. The content and notes are concise but comprehensive. (Educational Audio Visual Q1240)

Stage 26
The Grosvenor Museum, Chester, publishes two sets of six colour slides, one of museum exhibits including tombstones, and one of remains of Roman Chester.

Addresses of Suppliers

Archaeological Advisers Ltd, Park Street, Heytesbury, Warminster, Wilts
Educational Audio Visual Ltd, Mary Glasgow Publications Ltd, Brookhampton Lane, Kineton, Warwick CV35 0JB
Focal Point, 251 Copnor Road, Portsmouth, Hants PO3 5EE
The Grosvenor Museum, 27 Grosvenor Street, Chester CH1 2DD
Longman Group Ltd, Longman House, Burnt Mill, Harlow, Essex CM20 2JE
R. L. Dalladay, Harnser, Little Walden, Saffron Walden, Essex CB10 1XA
The Museum of Antiquities, The University, Newcastle upon Tyne NE1 7RU
Pictorial Colour Slides, 242 Langley Way, West Wickham, Kent
The Roman Baths Museum, Bath: order slides from Mementos, Stall Street, Bath, Avon.
The Slide Centre Ltd, 143 Chatham Road, London SW11 6SR
Viewtech AV Media, 161 Winchester Rd, Brislington, Bristol BS4 3NJ
Visual Publications, The Green, Northleach, Cheltenham, Glos GL54 3EX
H. A. B. White, 79 Teddington Park Road, Teddington, Middlesex

Unit IIIB

Introduction

The city of Rome provides the setting for Unit IIIB. Among the topics presented or touched on are the topography and physical appearance of the city, the contrast between the lives of rich and poor, social institutions such as the patron-client system, different types of public and private entertainment, the intense concern of many Romans for honour and status, the different ways in which philosophy and Christianity offered alternatives to the official state religion, and the struggle for prestige and power at the court of the emperor. The pupil's background material supplements the presentation in the stories.

The events of Stages 29 and 30 are set in September A.D.81; Stages 31 and 32 take place in 82, and Stages 33 and 34 in 83. A unifying link between the six stages of the Unit is supplied by the wealthy contractor Haterius and his family, while the presence of Salvius Liberalis in some of the stories provides continuity with earlier Units.

During this Unit, a number of passive forms of the verb are systematically introduced into the sentence patterns of the linguistic scheme. The range of ablative usages is extended in various ways, in particular by the introduction of ablative absolute phrases. Other new linguistic features include deponent verbs and the future tense.

A number of questions on comprehension and interpretation have, as in previous Units, been included in the pupil's text or suggested in the stage commentaries. Some of these questions, such as those in Stage 32, p. 74 of the pupil's text, are fairly demanding; others, such as those in Stage 33, p. 92, are sufficiently straightforward for pupils to tackle unaided even during their first reading of the passage; others again, such as those suggested in the commentary to Stage 29, p. 104 below, are designed to guide pupils to the meaning of complex sentences.

The manipulation exercises in the stages are of varying difficulty. The harder ones will be more suitable for oral work in class than for individual written work; alternatively an exercise can be partly or wholly worked through in class first, and set as written work afterwards.

As the stories become longer and the language increases in complexity, lesson planning becomes increasingly important. Not only does it lead to a more efficient use of the time available, but it also makes it easier to provide pace and variety within a single lesson or series of lessons. The following example shows how a sequence of lessons might be planned around 'Masada II' and 'arcus Titī' in Stage 29; the plan would naturally require adaptation to suit individual circumstances, and should also be subject to extempore modification in the classroom.

First lesson

1   Teacher puts *rūpēs, mūnītiōnēs* and *agger* on board for class to translate. Volunteer recapitulates story of Masada so far.

2   Read first two paragraphs of 'Masada II' (reading-aloud by teacher, followed by exploration by pupils, comprehension questions and translation, as described in Unit I Handbook pp. 18–21). Pupils read rest of story in pairs, then translate in class.

3   Discussion (subject to time available) of the Jews' reasons for committing suicide.

4   Teacher picks out sentences containing ablatives from 'Masada' (I and II) and puts them on blackboard for class to translate. Stress variety of translation. Refer class to pp. 4–5 of Language Information pamphlet for examples of ablative forms shown in paradigm.

5   Study the example at head of exercise 2 on p. 19.

Homework: revise 'Masada II', noting especially participles and subjunctives, and do exercise 2 as written work.

Second lesson

1   Pupils pick out subjunctives in third paragraph of 'Masada II', identify tense and say why subjunctive is being used. Teacher picks out some participles from 'Masada II': pupils identify type of participle, translate it and say which noun it describes.

2   Study photograph of potsherd on p. 12 of pupil's text. Discuss sources of our knowledge of events at Masada. Tell class about 1963–5 Masada excavation or read extract from translation of Josephus (see pp. 105–6 below).

3   Teacher puts on board some sentences from 'nox' and 'Masada' containing passive forms; translation (supplied by pupils) also written on board. Compare with corresponding sentences involving active forms; e.g. compare *Templum ā mīlitibus dīripiēbātur* with *mīlitēs Templum dīripiēbant*, written on board with its translation.

Homework: prepare 'arcus Titī I'.

Third lesson

1   Teacher gives back exercise 2 and practises any points that have caused trouble.

2   Class goes through 'arcus Titī I' answering teacher's comprehension questions and translating selected phrases and sentences. Part or all of 'arcus Titī I' read aloud by volunteer(s).

3   Discuss the description of the scene (see p. 108 below for suggestions).

4   Teacher picks out sentences in 'arcus Titī I' which contain passive forms; pupils translate. Study language note on passives.

5   Read first two paragraphs of 'arcus Titī II' (reading-aloud by teacher, followed by mixture of comprehension questions and translation).

Fourth lesson
1   Exercise 1 (p. 18 of pupil's text) orally.
2   Recapitulate on content of first two paragraphs of 'arcus Titī II', with supplementary questions such as 'What did a *corōna* look like? Where had the *candēlabrum* come from? What is the difference between *incēdere* and *ambulāre?*'
3   Study picture of procession on p. 15 of pupil's text (see p. 108 below for suggestions). Pupils read third and fourth paragraphs of 'arcus Titī II' in pairs or groups, then translate in class.
4   Read remainder of 'arcus Titī II' (various combinations of reading-aloud by teacher, exploration by pupils, comprehension questions and translation; brisk pace essential).
Homework: read Stage 29 background material.

It was suggested in the Unit I Handbook (p. 9) that in a four-year course Units IIIA and IIIB should normally constitute the second year's work; similarly, those with a three-year course should aim to finish Unit IIIB by the middle of the second year, in order to give pupils an adequate experience of reading original Roman authors, both adapted and unadapted, before beginning an external examination syllabus. Some or all of the following passages and exercises might be read quickly or omitted by those whose time allowance is short:

Stage 29   'Masada' I and II; exercise 4
Stage 30   'dignitās', lines 29–46; exercise 2
Stage 31   exercise 3
Stage 32   'philosophia', lines 14–38; exercise 2
Stage 33   'Tychicus'
Stage 34   'exitium I'; exercise 3

The practice of dividing a story into sections, each to be prepared by a different group of pupils (see Unit I Handbook, p. 23), may sometimes be useful to those who are short of time.

Study of social and historical topics

Unit IIIB's theme of *urbs Rōma* offers plenty of scope for the study of aspects of Roman civilisation. A discussion of appropriate teaching methods appears in the Unit I Handbook, pp. 26–7.

Both the Latin stories and the English background material supply pupils, directly or indirectly, with much factual information about aspects of Roman life. But there is more to historical studies than the acquisition of information; enquiry, analysis, inference, speculation, imagination and evaluation all have their place. The pupil's material is therefore designed to provide regular opportunities for considering such questions as the following:

1 Why were the facts as they were? e.g. 'Why were the markets close to the river?' 'Why did the public prefer *pantomīmī* to comedy and tragedy?'

2 What were the consequences of these facts? e.g. 'What would the senators have felt about an emperor who relied on ex-slaves in running the empire?' 'How would Domitian's building programme have affected (i) unemployment (ii) those who lived on main roads?'

3 What judgements of value or taste are suggested by the facts? e.g. 'Were the Jews at Masada right to prefer suicide to slavery?' 'Was the patron-client system a sensible one?' 'Would you have found a Roman banquet pleasant or disagreeable?' Discussions of this kind are generally more valuable if they include an attempt to see the situation through the eyes of the first-century participant as well as the twentieth-century observer; for example, if the question 'What do you think made the Jews prefer suicide to slavery?' is discussed first, a later question, 'Were they right?' will receive better-informed and better-judged answers.

4 How do we know? e.g. 'How do we know the arch of Titus was at the south-east end of the Forum?' 'How do we know what Nero did to the Christians?' This raises the crucial question of *evidence*. It is hoped that the previous discussion of the subject in Stage 28 will help pupils to pursue it further in Unit IIIB. It is hoped, too, that as well as working backwards from a statement in their text to the relevant evidence for the statement, whether literary, archaeological or epigraphic, pupils will sometimes be offered the chance to examine the problem the other way round, by looking at the evidence itself and attempting to draw conclusions from it under the guidance of the teacher. To this end, the pupil's material continues to include occasional quotations from the literary and epigraphic evidence. Literary evidence is at this stage usually presented in translated form; inscriptions are normally given in the original. To present the pupils with archaeological evidence for consideration is rather harder, for obvious reasons; it is sometimes possible, however, to view archaeological evidence on television, in a museum, or on a site, and the pupil's material itself includes a number of relevant photographs.

Filmstrip and cassette

Cambridge Classical Filmstrip 3, 'Rome', contains visual material
suitable for use with Unit IIIB. It includes the following topics:

- 1–11 Forum, arch of Titus and other monuments
- 12–16 Entertainment
- 17–26 Trade and corn supply
- 27–28 Insulae
- 29–31 Water supply
- 32–35 Death and burial

In this Handbook, reference to particular frames is given by filmstrip
frame number, and also (where appropriate) by slide number for the
benefit of those teachers who are using the slides which accompanied the
first edition of the course. Unless otherwise stated, references are to
Filmstrip 3 and Unit III slides.

A further filmstrip (Cambridge Classical Filmstrip 4) contains new
material, i.e. material not taken from the original slides. It includes
several frames of special relevance to Unit IIIB.

The second cassette accompanying the course includes the following
material from Unit IIIB:

- Stage 30 'dignitās'
- Stage 31 'salūtātiō' I and II
- Stage 32 'philosophia'
- Stage 33 'in aulā Domitiānī II'
- Stage 34 'īnsidiae'
-           'exitium'

Stage commentaries

Books are normally referred to by the name of their author. For details of title, publisher, etc., see Bibliography, pp. 172–4.

A list of the linguistic features introduced and discussed in each stage is given in the 'Linguistic synopsis of Unit IIIB' on pp. 160–1.

STAGE 29: RŌMA

Synopsis

Reading passages	Rome: the arch of Titus
Background material	the Roman forum
Language notes	3rd person singular and plural, present and imperfect passive
	purpose clauses with *quī* and *ubi*

Title picture

This shows the centre of Rome from the air. It will be useful for establishing the change of scene from Roman Britain in Unit IIIA. Pupils may already be able to identify some of the main buildings but might also return to this drawing later in their work on Rome, e.g. in connection with the map in Stage 31, p. 56.

Model sentences

The pupils' introduction to Rome begins with the *forum Rōmānum*; the pictures and captions seek to indicate something of its appearance and the part it played in the city's religious, political and social life. The forum is the subject of this stage's background material, and more information about the different buildings is given there, with a plan (p. 23). The arch of Titus, which stood on the Sacred Way leading into the forum, provides a theme for two of the stories.

The passive, hitherto met only in the perfect participle, now appears in its finite form. Examples are restricted to the 3rd person singular and plural of the present tense.

Apart from the names, the following words are new: *appellātur, summō* (new meaning), *ignis, Virginibus, extrēmō.*

nox

The events of Stage 29 take place in A.D.81, the year of the consulship of Flavius Silva who had captured the Jewish stronghold of Masada in A.D. 73. It was also the year in which Domitian succeeded his brother Titus after the latter's brief rule, A.D.79–81. Among his first actions was the building of an arch to Titus' memory. This, together with his other building schemes, was partly intended to attract to himself some of the popularity that had been enjoyed by his brother Titus and father Vespasian. For details of the inscription and carvings on the arch, see pp. 108 and 110 below. For the crane, see the background material of Stage 30, pp. 38–9.

The first story takes place on the night before Domitian's dedication of the arch. It touches briefly on the different layers of Roman society, the construction of the arch, the anxiety of Haterius and Salvius to finish the arch on time, and finally the desolation of the Jewish women prisoners.

Although Haterius himself is a fictitious character, the Haterii, with whom we have associated him, were an ancient Roman family who at one time possessed senatorial rank. They are thought to have built the magnificent tomb illustrated in the next stage.

The lament of the Jewish women is based on Psalm 22.1. It is adapted from the Vulgate translation, which reads: *Deus, Deus meus, respice in me, quare me dereliquisti?*

Pupils' experience of the passive is now extended to include the 3rd person forms of the imperfect. The illustration on page 7 of the pupil's text is intended to give help with lines 12–17 and 31–3 which contain a heavy vocabulary load and include examples of both the imperfect and present passive.

Lines 17–21 are difficult. After the teacher has read them aloud to the class, or after the pupils have read them through to themselves, they could be asked:

What was the Emperor Domitian intending to do to the arch?
What had been his feelings while Titus was alive?
What had he decided to do now that Titus was dead?
Whose favour did he want to win? What had their attitude been to
    Titus?

This use of simple comprehension questions has already been

recommended as a regular means of guiding pupils through major difficulties, see, for example, the Unit I Handbook, p. 20. Further examples of such questions are included in the Language Information pamphlet, p. 30. But this degree of help should only be given in difficult cases, and comprehension questions of this kind should always be followed later by translation and discussion. Here, for example, the lines should in due course be translated and pupils then be asked to explain the case of *vīvum* and *mortuum* and the point of *sibi*.

If pupils translate *nunc īnscrībuntur* (line 31) as 'are now inscribed', use *paene* in the previous sentence to establish that the arch is not yet finished, and thus encourage 'are now being inscribed'.

During this and the other stories in Stage 29, the main focus of attention from a linguistic point of view should be on the introduction of the passive forms and the consolidation of the ablative. A number of minor points also occur, such as the use of *nē* in the present story and of *dum* with the present indicative in 'arcus Titī II'. Answer pupils' questions on these if they ask about them, but detailed discussion can wait until they are picked up in the language note of a later stage or in the Language Information pamphlet. In practice, pupils often absorb these points with little difficulty, interpreting them from the context.

Masada

The story of Masada is told by one of the Jewish women prisoners to her son Simon, as they wait for dawn and death. Simon is determined to follow the example of his father who committed suicide at Masada.

The Jewish rebellion had raged for four years before it was ended by the capture of Jerusalem by Titus in A.D.70. The number of casualties on the Jewish side was enormous; the city was sacked, the Temple destroyed and in an effort to prevent any repetition of the revolt many of the survivors were driven out of the country and scattered among the cities of the empire. Titus returned to Rome with prisoners and the Temple treasure.

But Jewish resistance had not completely ended. A group of Zealots, led by Eleazar (Ben Ya'ir), established themselves at Masada, a fortress on a high flat-topped hill near the Dead Sea. From this base they harassed the Roman occupation forces for two years until in A.D.72 the commander of the Tenth Legion, Flavius Silva, who may have been related to Salvius, determined to wipe them out.

The story of what then happened is told in the pupil's text. It is based on our only source, the history of Josephus, who gives a vivid account of the final resistance at Masada, ending in the mass suicide of the defenders (*Jewish War* VII. 389–401). He may have talked to eye-witnesses and perhaps questioned the survivors, who hid themselves in a subterranean aqueduct (*specus* in the pupil's text) and then surrendered to the Roman soldiers. Yigael Yadin, who led the excavation of the site in 1963–5, demonstrated the general accuracy of Josephus' account and brought to light much evidence of the last days of Eleazar and his companions.

There is much helpful and interesting information about Masada in Yadin and in Pearlman. The filmstrip 'Masada' produced by R. Harker and others for Concordia Films (see Bibliography for address) is also strongly recommended. A tape-recording is available to accompany the filmstrip.

The coin on p. 9 is a sestertius from the mint at Rome. The inscription reads IVDEA CAPTA: 'The capture of Judaea'. SC (= SENATVS CONSVLTO: 'by the decree of the Senate') is a conventional slogan on Imperial coins, reflecting the usage of the late Republican magistrates.

The photograph of the rock of Masada on p. 10 shows the remains of the palace and fortifications that had been built by Herod the Great about 100 years earlier. Silva and his force of about 7000 legionaries and auxiliaries besieged the rock for six months in A.D.72–3. They built an encircling wall, some of which pupils may be able to pick out at the bottom right of the photograph, and eight camps. Two of these are on the photograph: the larger contained Silva's command headquarters. The ramp is clearly visible half-way along the right-hand side of the rock.

The potsherd shown on p. 12 is one of eleven small sherds, each bearing a single name, and unlike any others found on the site. It is thought possible that the other ten bear the names of the commanders who carried out the decision that the whole garrison be put to death rather than surrender to the Romans, and that these were the very sherds used at the end to decide which man was to kill the others and then himself.

The narrative shows the Romans from a hostile point of view. (The abusive description of Titus as Beelzebub in I, line 20 might be contrasted with the reference to him in line 20 of 'nox'.) It also shows the results of uncharacteristically inept provincial management by the Romans. There was a large failure on their part to understand Jewish culture and sentiment, and Roman governors displayed a mixture of antipathy and tactlessness which contributed to the final desperate bid for liberation. On the Jewish side there was a deep consciousness of national culture and religion which was allied, as it always had been, to political goals of freedom and independence.

For the plan of a possible sequence of lessons at this point, see p. 99–100 above.

The use of the ablative by itself to express means, method or cause was introduced in Stage 28 in the context of participial phrases, e.g. *vīnō solūtus*.

It is now also admitted to the main clause where it is kept close to the main verb, e.g.:

aedificia flammīs cōnsūmēbantur (line 22)
dux . . . rūpem castellīs multīs circumvēnit (lines 30–1)

The examples demonstrate how the idiomatic English equivalent may vary (' . . . by flames', ' . . . with many forts').

First language note (3rd person singular and plural, present and imperfect passive)

Invite pupils to compare the passive examples in paragraph 2 with the active examples in paragraph 1, and to comment not only on the verbs but also on the sentences as wholes. The question 'Is the meaning changed?' will often provoke valid comment, e.g. 'It's a different point of view', 'It's describing the same action in a different way'. Such comment is much more useful to pupils if they have produced it for themselves, than if it is merely handed out to them by textbook or teacher.

The terms 'active' and 'passive' have already been met in the context of perfect participles (pupils could be asked where they recall encountering the terms before), and the introduction of finite passive forms has been restricted to 3rd person singular and plural forms of the present and imperfect tenses, involving in effect only one novelty: the addition of *-ur* to the already-known active forms. Nevertheless, teachers should not be disconcerted if pupils need time and practice before they can consistently disentangle the various passive forms. In particular, some will at first be tentative over the correct translation of the tense of the passive; the difficulty here may not be to do with Latin at all, but spring from unfamiliarity with the corresponding English forms, for example the difference between 'was prepared' and 'was being prepared'.

arcus Titī

The procession, sacrifice and dedication are duly performed. The whole of Rome is on holiday. The only discordant note breaks in at the end when Simon rushes forward and completes the act begun by Eleazar and his comrades nine years before. These details, like the rest of the story of the Jewish survivors in Rome, are fictitious.

The ceremony is not, properly speaking, a triumph, but it has features in common with one. Invite pupils to suggest modern parallels and use their suggestions to bring out the several different aspects of the occasion: national (cf. Coronation, Guy Fawkes' Day); religious (cf. Christmas, Easter, Hannukah, Purim, Id al-Fitr); victory celebration (cf. the triumphal return home of F.A. Cup winners).

Some suggested questions on Part I

In what way does the Emperor intend to honour his dead brother today?
Where do the latecomers have to stand?
Which phrase suggests that many senators were insincere in their
enthusiasm to witness the ceremony?
In lines 9–12, how do the arrangements made for the senators differ
from those made for the equites? Suggest a reason for this.
What arrangements are being made to discover whether the intended
ceremony has the approval of the gods? (Pupils may be able to recall the
procedures of haruspices and augurs from Stage 23.)

If pupils translate *esset* (line 11) as 'was' or *īnspicerent* (line 17) as 'were
examining', use the context to guide them to a more appropriate
translation. Later, the use of the subjunctive in these sentences can be
discussed and the language note on p. 17 studied.

The first three paragraphs of Part II are linguistically straightforward.
They could be tackled by pupils working on their own with instructions to
draw up a complete list of the items in the procession, perhaps in
diagrammatic form, e.g. using labels and 'match-stick men'. The
procession itself was represented in sculptured form on the arch of Titus,
on the south side of the inner archway (left in the pictures on pp. 7 and
14): see filmstrip 4 (slide 22), and the drawing (based on the arch relief)
on page 15 of the pupil's text. Prominent is the Temple treasure, also
referred to on page 15; pupils should pick out the seven-branched
candlestick, the long trumpets and the sacred table. The tilted rectangular
objects are placards describing the treasure and giving details of the
successful campaign. The attitude of mind in which the Romans
approached such parades could be considered through the question, 'Why
was the Jewish treasure put on display?'

In Part II, Domitian appears in person. It may be helpful if teachers
supply some historical context at this point. Pupils might be told that
there were three Flavian emperors: Vespasian (reigned A.D. 69–79) and
his two sons Titus (79–81) and Domitian (81–96). Vespasian, whose part
in the Roman invasion of Britain was mentioned in Stage 15 p. 59 and
Stage 16 p. 72, was appointed to crush the Jewish revolt in 67; when he left
Judaea in 69 to launch his bid for the principate, Titus remained behind
to continue military operations as described above (p. 105).

The story can be used for practising the passive by means of a
'substitution' exercise, e.g. 'What does *sacrificātur* in line 23 mean? What
would *sacrificantur* mean? What would *sacrificābātur* have meant?'

Pupils might also be asked to pick out and translate some of the many
numerals in the stories of this stage.

Second language note (purpose clauses with quī and ubi)

After studying this note, pupils could be invited to compare such pairs of sentences as:

> *augurēs aderant quī cursum avium notābant.*
> *augurēs aderant quī cursum avium notārent.*

Manipulation exercises

Exercise 1   Type: vocabulary
            Linguistic feature being practised: compound verbs with *dē-*,
                ex- and *re-*

Pupils could also be asked to translate some assorted inflections of these verbs, e.g. *excurrō, reductus, dēpōnēbātur.*

Exercise 2   Type: transformation
            Linguistic feature being practised: imperfect subjunctive in
                purpose clause, introduced in Stage 26

The effect of replacing *ut* with *quibus* in sentence 4 might be discussed.

Exercise 3   Type: completion
            Missing item: participle
            Criterion of choice: sense and morphology
            Linguistic feature being practised: nominative and
                accusative, singular and plural, of present participle

The teacher could follow this by asking pupils to explain their choices or to identify the noun described by each participle.

Exercise 4   Type: transformation from English, using restricted pool of
                Latin words
            Linguistic features being practised: present participle, perfect
                active and passive participles, ablative singular and plural,
                relative pronoun

For some pupils, this exercise would be more suitable for oral work in class than for individual written work (see Introduction, p. 98). Encourage the habit of referring to the Language Information pamphlet in cases of doubt.

The background material

The pupil's material indicates the location and functions of some of the major buildings of the *forum Rōmānum*; it also suggests something of the forum's atmosphere and associations with Rome's history. Pupils should relate the reading material to the photograph and plan that accompany it, and refer where appropriate to the pictures and model sentences at the beginning of the stage. Filmstrip 1–9 (slides 19–22 and IV.28–9) also contain relevant material. Further description and illustration can be found in Dudley, Nash, and Platner and Ashby. Paoli 5–12 is informative and lively.

Additional notes on some of the features on the pupil's plan (p. 23): *Capitol*: the spiritual and emotional centre of Rome. If pupils know any of the associated legends, e.g. Tarpeia and the Tarpeian rock (Livy I.11) or the geese that warned of the Gallic invaders (Livy V.47), this will help to make the point that at the time of the Stage 29 stories, the Capitol was already a revered repository of religious and historical traditions stretching back over several centuries. On the summit was the temple of Jupiter Capitolinus, the focus of the state religion; its dominant position might be compared with that of the temple of Jupiter in the forum at Pompeii. The temple was burnt down during the civil war in A.D.69; Tacitus (*Histories* III.72) conveys very forcibly the emotional shock caused by this event. Its successor was itself burnt down in A.D.80 and was being replaced at the time of the Stage 29 stories. The potency of the Capitol as a symbol of Roman power and permanence was readily exploited by poets such as Virgil (*Aeneid* IX.448–9) and Horace (*Odes* III.30.7–9). Pupils who have visited Rome will remember the Capitol less for any classical remains than for Michelangelo's great Piazza del Campidoglio.

Basilica Iulia: the site of the Centumviral Court, specialising in inheritance cases, a great stamping-ground of the younger Pliny.

Rostra: the place where the heads of proscription victims such as Cicero were displayed (Plutarch *Cicero* 49).

Arch of Titus: covered with triumphal carvings and reliefs including the representation of the victory procession (see p. 108 above). A relief on the underside of the vault (not shown in our pictures but see filmstrip 5; slide 21) represents an eagle carrying Titus' soul to heaven. The inscription reads SENATVS / POPVLVSQUE ROMANVS / DIVO TITO DIVI VESPASIANI F(ILIO) / VESPASIANO AVGVSTO: 'The Senate and the People of Rome (dedicated this arch) to the deified Titus Vespasian Augustus, son of the deified Vespasian.' The elaborate bronze statue on the top, which shows Vespasian and Titus in a four-horse chariot, no longer exists.

Mention might be made of other sites with historical or legendary associations, such as the shrine of Venus Cloacina, where the Cloaca Maxima passes beneath the forum in front of the Basilica Aemilia (traditional site of the killing of Verginia by her father, described in Livy III.48) and the temple of Janus (exact location uncertain; possibly at the west end of the Basilica Aemilia) whose doors were ceremonially closed when the Romans were not engaged in any war.

STAGE 30: HATERIUS

Synopsis

Reading passages	Haterius the builder
Background material	buildings and building methods
Language notes	perfect and pluperfect passive

Title picture

This shows Haterius and his crane. The method of operating the crane is described on pp. 38–9 of the pupil's text. Note also the thin stripe on Haterius' toga and tunic which marks him as an eques.

Model sentences

These link the events of Stages 29 and 30. Haterius is at first euphoric at the praise heaped on his arch, then uneasy at the non-appearance of the promised reward. By the start of the first story in Stage 30, realisation of Salvius' deception has dawned, and Haterius' fury is bitter and intense. Pupils should be capable of producing appropriate comment on Haterius' last sentence.

The perfect passive is now introduced. In these sentences it is mainly restricted to the 3rd person singular, though a 1st person example is included near the end. Temporal adverbs such as *heri, hodiē, adhūc*, etc. have been freely employed to guide pupils to an appropriate translation ('was dedicated', 'was promised', 'was praised', followed by 'has been sent', 'have been deceived').

Suggestions for dealing with the perfect passive are given under 'First language note' on pp. 113–14 below. When handling the model sentences, it should normally be sufficient for the teacher to confirm that it is correct to translate *dēdicātus est* etc. as '*was* dedicated', etc. If the pupils are very able, or very dismayed at the apparently anomalous translation of *est*, some of the suggestions given for the language note could be used at this point, but normally it would be better to postpone them until pupils have met more examples of perfect passives in a connected context. There is no new vocabulary.

dignitās

Quintus Haterius Latronianus is not in the top echelon of society, but would very much like to be. He enjoys undoubted advantages. Related by marriage to the aristocratic Vitellii, he is also brother-in-law to the up-and-coming Salvius; in addition, he is a very successful building contractor. Socially, however, he belongs to one of the less distinguished branches of the Haterii family. Hence his agitation for a priesthood. He cultivates Salvius assiduously, and when he gets the contract to build the arch of Titus, he works desperately to win the honours which he imagines await him. Hence his bitter chagrin when the promised reward fails to appear.

Some pupils may ask how far the Haterius story is founded on fact. The reliefs on the Haterii tomb (illustrated on pp. 27, 33 and 37, and see notes on pp. 116–17 below) suggest that one member of the family worked as a builder, owned the giant crane whose representation appears on the tomb, and was involved in the construction of the arch of Titus, the Colosseum and other public buildings. The rest of the Haterius story is invention. For evidence connecting Salvius' wife Rufilla with the family of the Vitellii, see Stage 13, p. 15 of the pupil's text, and the Unit IIA Handbook, p. 11.

The aspirations that make Haterius so fretful illustrate the Romans' concern for *dignitās*. Personal prestige was a major goal in life; the notion that virtue is its own reward would not have commended itself to many Romans.

The theme, though important, is necessarily abstract, and the story is not an easy one to teach. One approach is to take the class through the dialogue on pp. 28–9 as quickly as possible, while making sure they are following the thread of the argument; alternatively, the class might work through the passage in groups, noting down the answers to the printed comprehension questions as they go but perhaps leaving till later the more complex questions 5 and 7. Subsequent discussion might centre on question 5. Pupils may be able to suggest modern parallels, in either the adult or the adolescent world, for sources and symbols of status.

The questions in the pupil's text can of course be supplemented by others. After the first two paragraphs have been read, questions 1 and 2 could be extended: 'What are the feelings of Salvius? of Haterius? Why could Haterius not sleep?' or, testing the pupils' memory of the events of the previous stage, 'Why should Salvius (in lines 6–7) be so pleased at the Emperor's praise of Haterius?' The implications of Vitellia's speech (lines 36–40) could be explored: 'Who is of higher social standing, Vitellia or Haterius? How is Haterius related to Salvius? What impression do you have of Vitellia's personality? What is the effect of the word order in lines 49–50?' A more speculative question might be raised at the end of the story: 'Why is it that Salvius, but not Haterius, gets what he wants as a result of the building of the arch?'

nōbilissimā gente depending on *nātam* (line 37) represents a further extension of ablative usages. Another small advance is the use of the present participle in the genitive without an accompanying noun (*grātulantium*, line 8). *maius* and *mīrābilius* (lines 51–2) provide an opportunity to comment on the neuter of the comparative adjective, referring if necessary to p. 9 of the Language Information pamphlet. Pupils have already met many examples of *melius* and *tūtius* with *est*; *suāvius* occurred in Stage 25 and *terribilius* in Stage 29.

This passage is on the cassette.

First language note (perfect passive)

By the end of 'dignitās' the pupils have met several examples of the 3rd person singular and plural of the perfect passive, also two examples of the 1st person singular. The language note adds the remaining persons.

Though the forms of the perfect passive are easily grasped, it will take most pupils time to become adept at translating them. *est* and *sunt* are by now so firmly associated with 'is' and 'are' that their occurrence with an apparently new meaning is liable to be a source of difficulty to some. Teachers can help by encouraging close attention to the context.

After the language note has been read, teachers might pick examples of perfect passives from the model sentences and from 'dignitās' and, reminding pupils of the context, ask them to recall the translation of these examples. Write the translation on the board, and invite comment. Pupils will ask, or even complain, about *est* and *sunt* in these examples. Confirm that it is the presence of the participle that is responsible for the 'new' translation of *est* and *sunt*. Elicit from the class that the participle is perfect; emphasis on this point usually seems to remove much of their initial puzzlement over the use of *est* and *sunt* in a past tense.

If pupils mistranslate this tense in their reading, translating *laudātus est*, for example, as 'it is praised', the most effective remedy will initially be through the context, e.g. by asking 'Do you mean the arch is *being* praised at the moment that Vitellia is speaking? Wouldn't that be *laudātur*, like the examples in Stage 29?' Later, remedial guidance can be based on the participle ('Look again; what sort of participle is next to *est*?' etc.).

A later lesson should consider the other difficulty in handling the perfect passive: the 'double' translation of, e.g., *portātus est* as 'has been carried' and 'was carried'. A comparison with the perfect active along the following lines may help: 'In Unit I, you learnt two ways of translating *parāvit*. Melissa, announcing that dinner is served, might say *Grumiō cēnam optimam parāvit*, meaning ... (Pupils: "Grumio has prepared ... " etc.) But somebody telling a story might say that Grumio was happy and so he ... (Pupils: "prepared ... " etc.) Similarly, there are two ways of translating the perfect passive. Melissa might announce the meal by saying "an excellent dinner *has been* prepared" but the narrator of a story would say "an excellent dinner *was* prepared".' Practise the point with some Latin examples, supplying contexts for the two types of translation.

polyspaston

Haterius adopts an unusual approach to the task of winning Salvius' support. Salvius is suitably impressed but remains evasive on the question of the priesthood. He does however satisfy Haterius' craving for *dignitās* by offering a smaller favour which Haterius readily accepts.

The behaviour of Glitus the foreman may be worth noting. At the start of the story he is relaxing, but the arrival of the boss with an important visitor galvanises him into activity, at least to the point of ordering the other workmen about.

Salvius' wish not to lose face before the *fabrī* might be elicited by asking 'Why did Salvius go pale? Why did he nevertheless sit on the beam? What is the relevance of the fact that the workmen were watching him?'

The panoramic view of Rome, on which Salvius comments in lines 22–4, could be related to pictures in the pupil's text, e.g. the title picture of Stage 29, or the map on p. 56, and features described by Salvius picked out on map or picture. Some of the filmstrip frames or slides mentioned on p. 123 below could be used here (see also Bibliography, p. 174).

Salvius lapses from his usual astuteness when he presents Haterius (in lines 25–6) with a chance to raise the question of a priesthood. But he recovers quickly, and adroitly diverts Haterius' attention from priesthood to *agellus*.

The dialogue between Salvius and Haterius has both a comic and a serious aspect . Once pupils have a clear picture of the physical circumstances, the comic element can be left to take care of itself. The serious element might be approached by asking 'Which of the phrases *alter spē immortālitātis ēlātus, alter praesentī pecūniā contentus* (lines 47–8) refers to Haterius, and which to Salvius?' Which would pupils prefer, *spēs immortālitātis* or *praesēns pecūnia*? Most will say '*praesēns pecūnia*' which leads easily to a further question: 'Why does Haterius seize so eagerly upon Salvius' offer? Is it reasonable to want to be remembered long after one's death?' Some alert pupils may point out that the wish of Haterius (or his real-life counterpart) was in fact granted: his monument does survive, and does commemorate his achievements. See notes on pp. 116–17 below.

The pluperfect passive is introduced in this passage. A language note follows. Pupils may tend to translate it as a perfect tense, e.g. by saying 'was prepared' for *parātum erat* (line 9). This should not be dismissed out of hand as wrong (English usage is more flexible than Latin in this respect), but pupils should be encouraged towards a more literal rephrasing.

Discussion might wait until after the final example has been reached (*datus erat*, line 42, which demands more obviously than the other examples an English pluperfect translation). Then, when the story has been completed, examples such as *parātum erat* might be re-examined, and those who were attracted by the translation 'was prepared' could be asked 'Do you mean "was *being* prepared"? If not, how could we make that clear in English?'

strepitū . . . plēna (line 5) is a further extension of ablative usage. For *labōrantium* (line 5), cf. *grātulantium* in line 8 of 'dignitās'.

Perfect and pluperfect passives could be practised by a substitution exercise in which different persons are substituted for the example in the text. For example: 'What did *admissī sunt* ('dignitās', line 9) mean? What would *admissī sumus* have meant? *admissus sum*?' Substitution of one tense for another should perhaps be left until pupils have met more examples of the pluperfect.

Second language note (pluperfect passive)

Pupils usually find this easier than the perfect passive. It therefore lends itself more conveniently to oral practice involving different persons and conjugations. To the examples in paragraph 3 might be added: *ductī erant*; *monitus erat*; *iussus erās*; *vīsī erāmus*.

Some pupils are helped by an analysis of the formation of this tense along such lines as: '*servātus* means "having been saved" and *erat* means "he was", so *servātus erat* means "he was (in a state of) having been saved", i.e. "he had been saved".'

Agreement between noun and participle, in respect of number and gender, might be discussed. After the stories and language notes have been read, pick out some examples of perfect and pluperfect passive forms from the stories, sticking at first to masculine forms. Invite comment on the singular and plural forms. Then pick out some examples of feminine and neuter singular forms, e.g. *parātum erat* and *fixa erat* in 'polyspaston', lines 9 and 10, and invite comment; finally the one example of a feminine plural (*audītae sunt* in 'dignitās', line 8) might be picked out and discussed. Later, the note on agreement in the Language Information pamphlet (page 17, paragraph 7) can be studied.

Manipulation exercises and further practice

Exercise 1   Type: vocabulary
            Linguistic feature being practised: nouns in *-itās*

Exercise 2   Type: transformation
            Linguistic feature being practised: accusative, genitive, dative and ablative, singular and plural

Extra help, if needed, can be supplied by telling pupils which word in the table of nouns provides the closest parallel to the noun in heavy type, e.g. *leō* for *legiō* (sentence 2), *cīvis* for *testis* (sentence 4) and *mercātor* for *flōs* (sentence 6). *māter* (sentence 8) has no exact parallel in the table, but if pupils are told it is third declension, that should be sufficient clue.

Further practice of the ablative morphology, in preparation for the introduction of the ablative absolute in Stage 31, can conveniently be carried out as a collaborative effort, in which the class turn simple prepositional phrases from English into Latin. Easy examples of adjectives and pronouns could be included as well as nouns.

Exercise 3 Type: completion
           Missing item: participle
           Criterion of choice: morphology
           Linguistic feature being practised: nominative and
               accusative, singular and plural, masculine and feminine, of
               perfect passive participle

Exercise 4 Type: transformation
           Linguistic feature being practised: pluperfect subjunctive
               with *cum*, introduced in Stage 24

It is important that pupils translate each pair of sentences before combining them, but not necessary for the translation to be written down. The exercise might be preceded by oral practice in forming 3rd person pluperfect subjunctives, both singular and plural, from a variety of perfect stems; pupils will find the transformation of the singular from *-it* to *-isset* easier than the transformation of the plural from *-ērunt* to *-issent*.

The background material

There is a wealth of reference material available on Roman buildings and building methods (e.g. Green, Hamey, Hodges, Landels and Macaulay), much of which is suitable for pupil reference. Where possible, building methods and materials should be studied in the context of actual buildings; for example, a slide of the interior of the Colosseum (filmstrip 16; slide 24) or of the Pont du Gard will spectacularly illustrate the principle of the arch.

The photograph on p. 37 shows part of the panel of buildings from the tomb of the Haterii. Pupils might enjoy picking out details of the very fine carving both here and in the part reproduced on p. 33. For example, the knot the workmen are tying at the top of the crane is clearly a reef-knot. Note here that the representation of the arch of Titus is not accurate but it can be identified from the inscription: ARCVS IN SACRA VIA

SVMMA: 'The arch at the top of the Via Sacra'. The figures in the arches are thought to be gods.

The eye, or hole, in the centre of the Pantheon dome (shown in the photograph on p. 40) is 9 m (nearly 30 ft) across and is the only source of light. The brickwork ring round it acts as the keystone for the vault. The concrete of the dome is in horizontal layers containing different materials; e.g. volcanic rock, which is comparatively light, was used towards the top. The square coffers (recesses) were originally enriched with stucco mouldings, painted and gilded. A bronze flower occupied the centre of every panel.

Suggestions for further work

1 'Imagine yourself as a member of Haterius' building squad and write a first-person account of the construction of the arch of Titus, including the final efforts to get it finished on time. Use the information in the stories and background material of Stages 29 and 30 and any other reference material available to you.'

2 With the aid of reference material such as the books mentioned above, pupils might be asked to research into particular building techniques (e.g. arch, vault or dome) or buildings (e.g. Pantheon, Colosseum) and present their findings in the form of a diagram, computer program or model. Those teachers who have experimented with classical model-making as an activity for their pupils have often been surprised at the painstaking care with which some quite unexpected pupils will research and construct their models. Where this does not fit easily into the normal programme of work, it is often feasible as an end-of-term project, in connection (for example) with an open day or similar exhibition.

STAGE 31: IN URBE

Synopsis

Reading passages }	{ the city of Rome
Background material }	{ patronage: patrons and clients
Language notes	ablative absolute
	purpose clauses and indirect command with *nē*

Title picture

This shows a boat unloading opposite the Tiber Island (see p. 57 of the pupil's text). The bridge in the background is the Pons Fabricius, which still survives (see filmstrip 20; slide 26).

Model sentences

A day in the life of waterfront Rome (cf. filmstrip 22; slide 41).

The ablative absolute is here introduced. Each ablative absolute phrase, except the last, is preceded by a finite version of the same event, e.g. *nautae nāvem dēligāvērunt* precedes *nāve dēligātā*. The ablative absolute phrases are temporal rather than associative, inviting translations introduced by 'When ...', 'As ...', 'While ...' and 'After ...'.

Concentrate on the subject-matter rather than the sentence-structure of these sentences, but pick out one or two of the ablative absolute phrases in passing, and put each on the board together with translations suggested by the class. Put up alternative versions, so that the idea of flexibility in translation is established at the very outset. Ask pupils the case of the words in these phrases. The case having been established as ablative, further discussion can wait until the first story has been read and more examples encountered.

If pupils have difficulty in translating the present participles, encourage them to use the clues in the picture (e.g. in picture 2 dawn has not yet broken, and in picture 3 the dockers are still working), or let the recognition of *illūcēscente, labōrantibus*, etc. as present participles meaning 'dawning', 'working' etc. lead to the translation 'was dawning', 'were working', etc.

The following words are new: *illūcēscēbat, saccāriī, expōnere, distribuit, occidere.*

adventus

This descriptive passage at first concentrates (like the model sentences) on the dockside, then on the Subura; the final paragraph introduces the theme of patron and client, which will be treated more extensively in the next story. The whole scene is viewed through the eyes of a newly arrived Greek girl, to be identified later as the philosopher Euphrosyne.

The map on p. 56 of the pupil's text should be used to locate the river and the Subura in relation to the forum. The background material might be used either as an introduction or as a follow-up to the story.

Some suggested questions

Why are so many people, rich as well as poor, up and about at this time of day? In what way is the status of the senators emphasised?

What activities are taking place by the Tiber? Where have the boats come from? Why were the granaries near the river?

Whose *adventus* is referred to in the title? Where is she going?

Why might the letter carried by the girl be important and what sort of things might you expect it to say (cf. Stage 26, where Quintus produces a letter of introduction from Barbillus)?

What sort of area does the Subura seem to have been?

Where were the beggars sitting? Why were crossroads (and also bridges) such favoured haunts of beggars?

Pick out two phrases which show the girl was unaffected by the workmen's behaviour to her.

Other possible points for discussion are the contrast between the lives of rich and poor (touched on in first and last paragraphs; remind pupils of the beginning of 'nox' in Stage 29) and the hazards of street life in the Subura (third and last paragraphs).

All recently introduced ablative usages are well represented in this story and the next. The following examples of ablatives with the main verb all occur in 'adventus':

multitūdine clāmōribusque hominum . . . obstupefacta est (lines 11–12).

puellam verbīs procācibus appellāvērunt (lines 17–18).

servī multitūdinem fūstibus dēmovēbant (line 25).

If pupils are still having difficulty with these usages, leading questions of the type 'What was she surprised by?' will help; this should be followed by further discussion of the example after the story has been completed.

salūtātiō

In Stages 29 and 30, Haterius appeared as a dependant of Salvius; we now see him from another standpoint, performing the role of patron to his own clients.

The story illustrates several features of the patron-client relationship: the *salūtātiō* or morning visit paid to patrons by clients; the *sportula* ('dole', 'handout'), once a little basket of food but now generally a handful of coins, dispensed casually among the crowd; the variety of small tasks required of clients by patrons, involving much standing about and waiting; the arrogance of the patron's slaves to the clients (cf. Juvenal V.63–75); the remoteness of the patron, who does not appear at the *salūtātiō* in person but operates through his *praecō*. On the patron-client theme, and especially the *salūtātiō*, Balsdon, *Life*, 21–4 has a helpful discussion. In exploring the topic with the class, elicit the mutual interdependence of patron and client: they need him for the *sportula*, but he needs them to accompany him about his business and run a multitude of errands, since this is an essential part of displaying publicly his wealth and status.

The story can be linked with the background material, and also with a selection from primary sources. See notes on p. 124 below.

The philosopher Euphrosyne is based on a historical figure mentioned in the following inscription, which was found in Rome:

EVPHROSYNE / PIA / DOCTA NOVEM MVSIS / PHILOSOPHA / V(IXIT) A(NNIS) XX   (*I.L.S.* 7783)

She is depicted as a young and attractive member of the Stoic school. She is also serious-minded and professional, visiting Rome for the first time, perhaps hoping to increase her own knowledge as well as to preach the merits of Stoicism. She is soon disappointed. Pupils may like to see her name written on the board in Greek script (Εὐφροσύνη) and be told its meaning ('Joy').

Question 3 in the pupil's text could be partly answered by a drawing. It could also be extended: 'Which Latin words used in the passage give us a clue to the herald's character? Does he behave in a way that the description of his character would lead us to expect? How is it that he, as a slave, can get away with treating Roman citizens in this way?' Question 5 is somewhat testing; the relevant details about nomenclature appeared in Stage 1, p. 11 and Stage 6, pp. 14–15. Question 6 is concerned with the rhetorical device of postponing till last the word or name which one's audience is most anxious to hear; pupils may be familiar with this device from various contexts – compères of variety shows, speeches of nomination at political rallies, etc.

In Part II of the story, the phrase *arbiter ēlegantiae* (line 16) might be explored. Once the idea has been established of somebody whose function is to monitor public taste and advise his employer accordingly, the role of Sunday colour supplements, fashion magazines, etc. might be compared. Eryllus appears in Stage 32. His role is based on that of C. Petronius, the *arbiter ēlegantiae* of Nero; pupils might be interested in Tacitus' account of his colourful life and death (*Annals* XVI. 18–19).

Euphrosyne's words to the slave in lines 26–7 are worth considering. Her advice is sensible and accords well with Stoic orthodoxy, but is unlikely to be persuasive. Pupils might be asked whether they, in the slave's position, would have preserved an *aequus animus*, and if not, whether this means Euphrosyne's advice was bad.

Part II is suitable for acting or reading aloud. Four readers are required: narrator, slave, herald, Euphrosyne. Both parts are on the cassette.

From this and the previous story, examples of the passive should be picked out and practised; in particular, the different tenses should be compared. For example, the class could be asked 'What did *reficiēbantur* ('adventus', line 16) mean? What would *reficiuntur* mean? *refectī erant*? Give two translations of *refectī sunt*.' It is important that pupils should be secure in handling these forms, as they are about to meet them again in the different context of deponent verbs.

First language note (ablative absolute)

Teachers may wish to tackle this lengthy note in instalments, parhaps paragraphs 1–3 in one lesson, and paragraph 4 in another.

Use the examples to practise flexibility of translation. For instance, when studying *duce interfectō* (sentence 4 of paragraph 3) pupils should be able to produce 'When their leader was killed', 'Since their leader had been killed', 'After the killing of their leader', etc. Using an example such as sentence 5 of paragraph 3, raise the possibility of translating with an *active* perfect participle ('Having heard the shouts', etc.). Remind the class of any previous discussion of the question 'If *parātus* means "having *been* prepared", how did the Romans say "having prepared the dinner"?' (see the Unit IIIA Handbook, p. 18).

The ablative absolute's independence of the main structure of the sentence, illustrated implicitly in paragraph 1 of the note, is best explained by practical demonstration. Invite pupils to read out the ablative absolute phrases in paragraph 3; then invite others to read out the examples in paragraph 3 *omitting* the ablative absolute. Use such questions as 'Does it still make sense without the ablative absolute?' and 'Is it a complete sentence?' to establish the point that the ablative absolute is not connected structurally with the rest of the sentence. Reinforce the point if need be by referring to the word *absolūtus* ('detached') from which the construction takes its name.

Manipulation exercises

Exercise 1   Type: vocabulary
            Linguistic feature being practised: compound verbs with
               ab-, *circum-* and *in-*
Further practice in compound verbs could include:

discēdere (go away)	*dīmittere*
percurrere (run through)	*perrumpere*

convocāre (call together)	*convenīre, compōnere*
trānsmittere (send across)	*trānsīre, trānscurrere*
prōpōnere (put forward)	*prōcēdere, prōcurrere, prōferre*

Those pupils who have now grasped the principle behind compound verbs should be given an encouragement and a warning: confirm that the meaning of an unfamiliar compound verb can often be deduced from its component parts, especially the 'verb' part; but emphasise that this principle should be used as a clue rather than an infallible guide, since the meaning of the parts, especially the preposition, is not always strictly predictable in compounds. The point can be conveniently illustrated from *āmittere* and *invenīre*.

Exercise 2 Type: completion
Missing item: verb
Criterion of choice: morphology
Linguistic feature being practised: 3rd person singular and plural, present and imperfect passive, introduced in Stage 29

In sentences 2, 3, 5 and 6, there is a deliberate variation of number (singular subject with plural agent, or vice versa) to reinforce the point that the nominative, and not the agent, controls the number of the verb. If pupils get this wrong, producing for example *oppugnābantur* for sentence 5, an appropriate response might be 'Look again: you're thinking of sentences like *barbarī oppidum oppugnābant*, where the sentence was about the barbarians and what they did, and so the verb was active; this time the verb is passive, and the sentence is about the town and what was done to it.'

Exercise 3 Type: completion
Missing item: noun *or* verb *or* participle
Criterion of choice: sense and syntax
Linguistic feature being practised: sentence structure

Second language note (purpose clauses and indirect command with nē)

Several examples of these constructions with *nē* have occurred in recent stages. Encourage pupils to experiment with different ways of translating the examples in paragraphs 2 and 3. The examples in paragraph 2 could be compared to the corresponding direct commands *nōlī nāvigāre, nōlīte līberōs interficere*, etc.

The background material

The material on the city of Rome could conveniently be taken immediately before or after reading 'adventus', and the material on patronage postponed until 'salūtātiō' has been read.

The city of Rome

The area and population of Rome in the 1st century A.D. are matters of controversy among scholars. The figures in the pupil's text depend on a disputable assumption that the city's population spilled only slightly beyond the area of 20 square km (7¾ square miles) demarcated by the toll-posts. Even if this assumption is mistaken, the point made by the comparison in the pupil's text is not significantly affected. The Los Angeles and Greater Manchester statistics are for 1976 and 1983 respectively.

The class might consider some of the reasons why the massive overcrowding in first-century Rome could not be relieved by expansion. It had been found impracticable to allow *insulae* to rise very high because they were liable to sudden collapse or disastrous fires: Augustus had fixed the limit at 21 m, 70 ft (cf. p. 41 of Stage 30). The other solution, expansion outwards in the form of the large suburban residential areas which are such a feature of modern cities, is not practicable without modern forms of transport.

The places mentioned in the pupil's text should be related not only to the map on p. 56 but also, wherever possible, to photographs. These can be either slides (e.g. filmstrip 1–20; slides 19–26 and IV. 28–9) or such photographs as those in Dudley, Scherer, Nash, or Van der Heyden and Scullard. Pictures of reconstructions, such as those in Sorrell and Birley, can be extremely helpful. Photographs and postcards of the older quarters of present-day Rome (like the photograph on p. 57) can illustrate features of the ancient city which still persist: high buildings, for example, sometimes built around internal courtyards, and narrow streets teeming with life.

The map on p. 56 has deliberately been simplified to show only the main features mentioned in the text. Pupils may need to be reminded that the whole area was filled with many buildings of all kinds.

At the end of the first century there were nearly a dozen aqueducts bringing water into the city of Rome. The Aqua Claudia, shown in the photograph on p. 59, was 74 km (46 miles) long, but only about 14 km (9 miles) was raised on arches. It was considered one of the best sources of water and so was taken to the palaces on the Palatine.

This photograph and that on p. 100 (and filmstrip 1 and 13) show parts of the large reconstruction model ('plastico') of Rome at the time of Constantine. It was made in 1937–8 and is now in the Museo della Civiltà Romana.

The more the pupils associate each place with its functions, the more vividly will they imagine it. They might therefore be asked: If you had been a first-century Roman, where would you have gone ...

... to give thanks after recovering from fever? (temple of Aesculapius on Tiber Island)

... for a cheap haircut? (Subura)

... for a summer evening stroll away from the crowds? (Campus Martius)

... to watch a chariot-race? (Circus Maximus)

... to hear an open-air political speech? (Rostra in forum)

Similar examples can readily be added. The answers given are not of course the only possible ones.

Invite the class to list as many ways as they can in which the lives of the rich differed from those of the poor in first-century Rome; they should make use of what they have read in the stories and background material, supplemented by any additional information they possess. The contrasts might include: food (banquets of rich in 'nox' – meagre meals obtained by poor with *sportula*); housing (mansions and palaces of rich – *īnsulae* of poor); water (rich connect with main water supply – poor use fountains); summer residence (rich escape to *vīllae rūsticae*, like Haterius, Stage 30, p. 28 – poor stay put in hot unhealthy city). This would link very easily with a reading of parts of Juvenal *Satires* III.

The possibilities for pupil research on the topic of city life are vast, though dependent on the time available. Some information could be ferreted out by pupils for themselves; some would require teachers' guidance. There is useful material in Carcopino 13–64, Cowell 13–34, Dilke, Frederiksen (in Balsdon (ed.) *Roman Civilisation* 151–68), Leacroft, Meiggs 235–51 (an important description of *īnsulae*), Nash, Paoli 1–53, and Platner and Ashby. The theme can also be pursued, under guidance, in translations of literary evidence:

1 police and fire patrols (Justinian *Digest* I.xii.1, xv.3; Lewis and Reinhold II.26–8)
2 Augustus' building programme (Suetonius *Augustus* 28.3–30.2; Lewis and Reinhold II.67–9)
3 aqueducts (Frontinus *The Water Supply of Rome* II.98–129; Lewis and Reinhold II.69–72)
4 dimensions of city (Pliny *Natural History* III.v.66–7; Lewis and Reinhold II.222)
5 utilities and amenities (Strabo *Geography* V.iii.8; Lewis and Reinhold II.223–4)
6 the great fire (Tacitus *Annals* XV.38–44; Lewis and Reinhold II.224–7)
7 baths (Lucian *The Bath* 4–8, and Seneca *Moral Epistles* LVI.1–2; Lewis and Reinhold II.227–8)
8 life in Rome (Juvenal *Satires* III; Lewis and Reinhold II.239–42)

The quotation in the pupil's text is adapted from Juvenal *Satires* III.243–8.

Patronage

The story 'salūtātiō' has portrayed the commonest type of Roman patronage: the distribution of *sportula*, on behalf of a wealthy patron, to his dependent clients. The background material provides further information about this and other types of patronage, which operated not merely at the level of the poor and needy but across the whole spectrum of Roman society. Pupils may be able to quote modern examples of patronage (probably more familiar as 'sponsorship'), e.g. of sport or the arts.

The following is a selection of source material relevant to points mentioned in the text:

Horace *Satires* I.6.54–64 (introduction to Maecenas; cf. *Letters* I.16.1–16 for the Sabine farm)
Pliny *Letters* VI.23 (Cremutius Ruso to speak with Pliny in court)
Pliny *Letters* II.9 (candidature of Sextus Erucius)
Pliny *Letters* IV.1 (donation of temple to Tifernum)
Pliny *Letters* IV.13 (contribution to schoolmaster's salary at Comum)
Martial *Epigrams* VI.88 (punishment for not addressing patron as '*domine*')
Juvenal *Satires* V.24–155; Pliny *Letters* II.6; Martial *Epigrams* I.20, III.60 (graded dinner-parties).

Translations of some of this source material could be duplicated and presented to the class for interpretation and discussion.

Pupils should be encouraged to notice connections between the different topics they study. Here, for instance, Maecenas' gift of the Sabine farm might be linked to earlier discussion of the *vīllae rūsticae* owned by the rich (see p. 124 above); and the patron-client relationship could be compared to the Roman view of the relationship between gods and man, described in Stage 23.

Patronage might also be contrasted with another important Roman institution: *amīcitia*. Patronage flows from higher social status to lower; *amīcitia* exists between social equals. (A tactful patron might blur this distinction by referring to the recipients of his patronage as his *amīcī*.)

Suggestions for discussion

It may be useful to attempt an assessment of the uses and abuses of the system. Divide the blackboard into two columns, 'pro' and 'con', and invite the class to contribute their views, supported as far as possible by examples taken from the stories and background material. Arguments in favour might include: support for the humbler citizen in the law-courts, protection against personal economic disaster, and financial help for the needs of the community, as provided by Pliny for Comum. The arguments against include: hypocrisy, advancement by personal influence, lack of incentive to get on by one's own efforts, the patron's exploitation of his clients. On occasion, the very basis of a patron-client relationship (protection in exchange for services) could be abused. The withholding of 'protection' can be a potent threat: the 'services' of one's dependants can be put to sinister uses. In its least savoury aspects, the patron-client system foreshadows the mafia.

2   The analysis above might lead to a comparison between Roman and modern systems of social security. Pupils will have had too little experience to develop it very far, but some aspects should be accessible to them. For example, 'Do people today depend on others as a client did on a patron? What are the ways in which the community today helps people in need? Which kinds of needs are the responsibility of our departments of social welfare? Do you think that, especially in a city, there are advantages in knowing people to whom one can go for advice and help?'

Words and phrases checklist

This might be a convenient moment to study the paradigm of *īdem* on p. 12 of the Language Information pamphlet. For some suggestions see p. 155 below.

STAGE 32: EUPHROSYNĒ

Synopsis

| Reading passages | } | { Roman society |
| Background material | | philosophy and other beliefs |

Language notes	deponent verbs
	gerundive of obligation (with transitive verbs)
	future participle

Euphrosynē revocāta

The story of Euphrosyne's recall offers several possibilities for discussion:
1 Why does Euphrosyne at first fail to gain admission? Possible answers: the private feud between Eryllus and the *praecō*; the power wielded by the *praecō* at the *salūtātiō*; the practice, evidently normal, of gaining an entrée to the patron's house through bribery.
2 Why has Eryllus sent for a philosopher? It transpires that she is to provide entertainment at the birthday party. Neither Eryllus nor Haterius evinces the slightest interest in philosophy as such; Eryllus' second speech makes it clear he has summoned Euphrosyne because philosophy is fashionable. Teachers may here wish to use some of the material below on philosophers.
3 Why does Haterius agree to Eryllus' suggestion of a philosopher? He suspects all philosophers of being stern and gloomy, but when Eryllus promises a philosopher who is both young and female, doubts vanish and he becomes enthusiastic.

The background material (p. 81) contains examples of questions inquired into by Greek and Roman philosophers. Others could be added: 'What is justice?' 'How should a city be governed?' 'How can we tell truth from falsehood?' and above all 'How ought men to behave?' In first-century Rome, the philosopher was not only (or not at all) a contemplative inquirer but a public entertainer, sometimes performing literally on the street-corner, where he combined the roles of guru and busker in a manner not unlike the modern TV pundit. Rome's attitude to philosophers veered erratically between enthusiastic interest and violent hostility, with periodic mass expulsions. No doubt some Romans dismissed philosophy as nonsense, and preferred to live their lives by pragmatic and materialistic standards rather than lofty ethical ideals. Furthermore, philosophy was often politically suspect; it supplied ideological backing for opponents of the principate (see p. 82 of the pupil's material). Pupils may recall, from Stage 26, p. 109, how Agricola told his son-in-law that his own youthful interest in philosophy had been firmly squashed by his mother. But in A.D.82, the year in which this stage is set, Epictetus, the famous Stoic, was teaching in Rome and for the moment philosophy was in favour.

Deponent verbs now appear in their finite form. The first four examples are accompanied by line drawings and glossed; all four have already been met in participial form. With the aid of these clues, together with the story-line and the teacher's comprehension questions, pupils are often able to take the new feature in their stride. In practice, they rarely mistranslate a deponent verb as if it were passive, since many examples either are intransitive or govern a very obvious object. When pupils themselves begin to notice and comment on the new feature, confirm their observations where appropriate, answer their questions, and let discussion develop; but the initiative should come from the pupils rather than the teacher.

All examples of deponent verbs in this story are in the perfect tense and nearly all are in the third person. After the first four examples, they are left unglossed in the pupil's text if they have previously been met in participial form. The first-person form *adeptus sum* (lines 29–30) has been glossed; notice how pupils cope with the unglossed *adeptus es* a few lines later.

cēna Haterii

Haterius' dinner-guests are a very mixed lot. Some are wealthy but lowborn; others are nobly-born but poverty-stricken. The presence of the consul Sabinus is something of a coup for Haterius, whose longings for social advancement should be remembered by pupils from Stage 30. Haterius flatters the consul sedulously, though he ineptly places himself, and not Sabinus, in the place of honour. For a diagram of the placing of dinner-guests, see Stage 2, p. 12; and for further information on this and other details of Roman dinner-parties, see Balsdon, *Life* 32–53 and Paoli 92–9.

Some details of the dinner are taken from Petronius, *Cena Trimalchionis*. Haterius' eagerness to impress his guests results in a vulgar display. Pupils might be asked 'What impression of himself is Haterius trying to present to his guests? By what methods does he seek to do this?' Answers might include the bright-coloured and costly Tyrian cushions, the bejewelled golden rings, the silver toothpick, the gimmick of the stuffed boar, the pretentiously labelled wine, and Haterius' boastful and elaborate introduction of Euphrosyne. Pupils could then be asked whether all this makes a favourable impression on *them*; if not, why not? They will perhaps be able to suggest present-day examples of ostentatious attempts to impress neighbours.

The class will now be very familiar with the use of comprehension questions to explore a passage, and might usefully try to devise some of their own; each pupil might be required to compose up to three questions on lines 6–20 of the story to be answered by a neighbour. Some rules will be needed, e.g. that each question must be answerable, that the composer of the question must know the answer, and that the question must either be answerable from the text or (if it is a 'general knowledge' question, e.g. 'what was a consul?') arise directly from a reference in the story.

Deponent verbs continue to be practised; examples of the imperfect and pluperfect tenses are now included.

First language note (deponent verbs)

This note deals with the three tenses of deponent verbs which have
already been met in the stories (imperfect, perfect and pluperfect) and
adds the present tense. This is of course an easy extension in view of the
similarity of its formation to that of the imperfect; and the relevant
inflections have already been met in the present passive forms of
'ordinary' verbs.

Only the 3rd person forms are included in this note. These are the only
forms of the present, imperfect and pluperfect tenses of deponent verbs to
appear in Stages 32–4. The forms of the perfect tense in these stages
include occasional 1st and 2nd person examples, whose meaning is
readily established from the context and by analogy with the 3rd person
forms and the perfect passive. The perfect and pluperfect tenses of
deponent verbs are given in full in the Language Information pamphlet.

Pupils may need some help with the final examples in paragraph 3,
which have no supporting context. Encourage them to refer back to
paragraph 2 if they are hesitant about the tense. Practise the contrasts
between singular and plural (*ingreditur – ingrediuntur; secūtus erat – secūtī
erant*) and between 3rd person singular masculine and feminine in the
perfect and pluperfect (*profectus erat – profecta erat*).

The language note is best tackled in instalments: paragraphs 1–3 in one
lesson, paragraphs 4 and 5 in another. Paragraphs 4 and 5 make the point
that pupils have already had a lengthy experience of deponent verbs in
their perfect participial form. The distinction between perfect active and
perfect passive participles, familiar since Stages 21 and 22, is re-expressed
in the context of deponent and 'ordinary' verbs. The examples in
paragraph 5 should be translated. They can then be used to elicit the
point that there is nothing about the *form* of a perfect participle to make it
active or passive (e.g. the active *cōnātus* has the same ending as the passive
parātus); what matters is whether the verb is deponent or not (e.g. *cōnātus* is
active because it comes from a deponent verb, *parātus* is passive because it
comes from an 'ordinary' verb).

philosophia

Some suggested questions

Does Sabinus (line 4) really not know what a poor man is? If he does
know, why does he ask?

Why are the guests startled (*obstupefactī*) by what Euphrosyne says in
lines 14–15? Do you think her words are deliberately aimed at Haterius?
(The latter question has no clear-cut answer. Euphrosyne's naive manner

in telling her fable might suggest that her remark here is an innocent
blunder, but her parting shot in line 55 hints at a rather sharper persona.
The point could be reconsidered later in a general discussion of
Euphrosyne's personality and attitude.)

For what qualities does Euphrosyne praise the 'hero' of her story? Do
you think it is just a coincidence that he is a country-dweller and not a
townsman? (This could lead to a discussion of some of the virtues
attributed to country life by traditionally minded Romans; for instance,
the peasant-farmer's disregard of honour and riches, and his piety
towards the gods, who affect his life more directly than the city-dweller's.
Pupils might at this point study the illustration of the peasant-farmer on
p. 73 noting for example the wayside shrine at the top left. Note also the
lambs slung across the cow and the pig hanging from the pole on his
shoulder.)

Why does Rabirius try to prevent Sabinus from making advances to
Euphrosyne ('*nōlī eam tangere!*' line 46)?

What does Haterius try to do during the brawl? What had been his
original intentions in holding the party?

The questions printed in the pupil's text are open-ended and so allow a
variety of opinions. They could be tackled independently of the teacher,
with the class divided into half a dozen groups. Let some groups tackle
question 1 and others question 2, before the whole class comes together for
discussion under the teacher's direction.

Question 1. Pupils will already have realised that Euphrosyne and her
audience are completely at cross purposes. She thinks they want to learn
about Stoicism; their comments make it plain their interest lies elsewhere.
For the kind of dinner entertainment they might have been expecting, cf.
the Stage 16 model sentences, the dancing-girls of Juvenal, *Satires*
XI.162–4 or the vulgar buffoons of Pliny, *Letters* IX.17. Euphrosyne also
fails to present her theme in a way that might gain the attention of her
audience. She presents her sermon in story form (an approach that the
pupils will have experienced at first hand in school assembly), but her
manner is naive and didactic. In any case, the way of life presented in her
story has nothing in common with the life-style of her listeners.

Question 2. Harder than Question 1. Are the satisfactions of self-
sufficiency, a clear conscience, and achievement through hard work,
deeper than the satisfactions of material possessions? Are they sufficient
compensation for the misfortunes of the poor man? Euphrosyne's paradox
(lines 34–5) is expressed more sharply in Epicurus' aphorism (consistent
with Stoicism as well as Epicureanism) that the wise man is happy even
on the rack (Diogenes Laertius, *Lives of Philosophers* X.118).

The story is suitable for reading aloud. Seven readers are required:
narrator, Euphrosyne, Sabinus, Apollonius, Baebius, Rabirius and

Haterius, with optional crowd noise from the rest of the class. It is also on the cassette.

If pupils have difficulty with Euphrosyne's last remark, take them through *ēn Rōmānī, dominī orbis terrārum* first, then ask which word in the final phrase makes a contrast with *dominī*, and when they have located *servī*, ask 'What does she say the Romans are slaves of?' Idiomatic translations of *ventris Venerisque servī* can then be invited.

All three stories in Stage 32 provide opportunities for revising the subjunctive. The class could be asked to pick subjunctives from the text and say why the subjunctive has been used in each instance.

Second language note (gerundive of obligation with transitive verbs)

Pupils have been meeting the gerundive in such sentences as *mihi effugiendum est* for some time now, and should have little difficulty in making the transition to such sentences as *nōbīs nāvis reficienda est*. Discussion of the use of *est*, and the agreement between noun and gerundive, should wait until more examples have been met (see under 'Language Information pamphlet', p. 157 below).

Manipulation exercises and further practice

Exercise 1   Type: vocabulary
            Linguistic feature being practised: verbal nouns in -*tus*, -*sus*
If the teacher wishes to add that nouns of this kind all belong to the fourth declension, the point should not be left as an abstraction, but demonstrated in a practical way, e.g. by referring to the paradigm of *manus* on p. 4 of the Language Information pamphlet and asking pupils the Latin for 'groans', 'songs', 'about the arrival', 'about the return', etc.

Exercise 2   Type: sentence composition from pool of Latin words
            Linguistic features being practised: nominative, accusative
                and genitive, singular and plural; 3rd person singular and
                plural of imperfect and perfect
This is the first time the genitive has been included in an exercise of this type. Pupils might be allowed to add further items at the teacher's discretion, e.g. *intereā*, *subitō* or other adverbs, or such prepositional phrases as *in carcere*, *prope templum*, etc.

Exercise 3   Type: completion
            Missing item: adjective
            Criterion of choice: morphology
            Linguistic feature being practised: agreement of noun and
                adjective

Pupils may need reminding that there are three ways in which an adjective must agree with a noun, and that agreement does not necessarily mean identity of ending. They might be asked why *līberālem* is the right answer in the example that precedes the exercise.

Exercise 4 Type: transformation
Linguistic feature being practised: imperfect subjunctive in indirect command, introduced in Stage 27
Specific points practised include the 1st and 3rd persons of the imperfect subjunctive, positive and negative commands, and the use of *sē* to refer back to the original speaker. To balance these demands on the pupil, generous help has been given with the formation of the imperfect subjunctive in the first four questions; but in questions 5 and 6 pupils have to execute more of the transformation for themselves.

This stage would be a suitable time to begin consolidation work based on the 'About the language' section of the Unit IIIB Language Information pamphlet. See pp. 154–9 below for commentary.

Third language note (future participle)

Pupils should by now be sufficiently familiar with participles to make appropriate comment on the new feature for themselves. Ask why *cōnscēnsūram* and not *cōnscēnsūrus* is used in the third example in paragraph 1. Encourage variations on 'about to . . . ' and 'going to . . . ', e.g. 'on the point of . . . ' and (with *esset* in indirect questions) 'would . . . ' Pupils should also be able to offer their own comments on the differences in form between perfect and future participles, set out in paragraph 3, and translate further examples of future participles, e.g. *scrīptūrus, discessūrus, pugnātūrus.*

The background material

Roman society

Pupils often ask what would be the modern equivalent of sums of money such as those mentioned in the text; but the difference between ancient and modern conditions makes comparison impossible. It is useless to equate (say) the cost of a bushel of wheat in the first century with its cost in the twentieth, or the earnings of a Roman legionary with those of his modern counterpart, because such equations depend on unprovable assumptions about the economic context, e.g. that the average first-century Roman spent on wheat the same proportion of his total personal expenditure as does the average twentieth-century Englishman. Useful comparisons can, however, be made *within* the first-century context. A client collecting sportula on 100 days of the year would receive 625 sesterces (HS.) each year from this source. A labourer's daily wage is often estimated, by a rather hazardous inference from *Matthew* 20.2, at 4 HS., in which case a labourer working 200 days in a year would earn 800 HS. in that time. When we look at the upper end of the scale, the figures in the ancient evidence usually denote capital; for purposes of comparison with the less well-off, they need to be converted into income. If (following Carcopino 79) we assume an interest rate of 5%, the 400,000 HS. which constituted the property qualification of an *eques* would bring in 20,000 HS. each year – an income evidently regarded as modest but comfortable by Juvenal (*Satires* IX.139–41 and XIV.322–6). The senatorial capital of 1 million HS. would bring in 50,000 HS. p.a. Pliny, who described himself, truthfully or otherwise, as 'not rich', had a capital of about 20 million HS. (income p.a. 1 million HS.), and his rival Regulus had three times as much. At the extreme were exceptional cases like Seneca (capital 300 million HS.) and Narcissus (400 million HS.). For further details, see Balsdon, *Life* 354 and Carcopino 79–81. From all these figures, a picture emerges of a dramatic disparity between rich and poor in Roman society. Pupils might discuss these inequalities, and consider how far poverty was alleviated by the patron-client system; they might compare the role of taxation as a present-day method of reducing inequalities.

The exact qualifications for membership of the *ōrdō senātōrius* and the *ōrdō equester* were extremely complicated, and the account in the pupil's text deliberately omits some of the complexities. If pupils ask about the difference between the *ōrdō senātōrius* and the Senate, it should be enough to say that a member of the sentaorial class was not entitled to sit in the Senate unless and until he had reached the office of *quaestor*; an account of the *cursus honōrum* containing more information on this and other aspects of the senatorial career appears in Stage 37.

Two important sections of Roman society, freedmen and women, are not discussed in the pupil's text at this point but are dealt with in Stage 34 and Stage 38 respectively.

Encourage pupils to link the present material with that on patronage, and to think of ways in which patronage might enable people to move up the pyramid. Pliny's gift to Romatius Firmus (*Letters* I.19), enabling him to become an *eques*, provides one example; the bestowal of the *lātus clāvus* by the emperor provides another. Among equestrians who refused promotion were Maecenas and Atticus in the first century B.C., and the men mentioned in Pliny, *Letters* I.14, III.2. Invite the class to suggest reasons for such refusals. Possible answers include a desire to avoid the risks and toils of a political career at the higher level, or a preference for being a prominent *eques* rather than an undistinguished senator, or a wish to pursue an active commercial career, from which senators were barred by law and social convention.

The reference in the pupil's text (p. 80) to 'casual and irregular employment' might be further explored. There was clearly an immense need for porters in Rome, especially in view of the restrictions on wheeled traffic (Stage 31, p. 59), and pupils should be able to suggest examples, such as dockworkers, luggage-carriers, *aquāriī* and sedan-chair bearers. They might also recall some of the massive building projects mentioned earlier (Stage 30, p. 41), and this could lead to discussion of the role of the emperor as a provider of employment (cf. Suetonius, *Vespasian* 18).

Astrology, philosophy and other beliefs

On philsophy generally and Stoicism in particular, some of the material on pages 127 and 130 above might be used here. Teachers could refer to the use of 'stoic' in English for someone who endures pain or misfortune bravely and uncomplainingly. The reference to Virtue as 'burnt by the sun' may need explanation; pupils may associate sunburn with lolling lazily on a beach rather than toiling in the heat of a Mediterranean day. The Romans' association of *umbra* with *ōtium* could be mentioned, and illustrated from the drawing of Haterius at the beginning of the stage.

The Stoic tradition that Epictetus' lameness was caused by brutal treatment represents him as calmly saying to Epaphroditus, 'If you go on doing that, you'll break my leg', and a moment later, equally calmly, 'I told you so'. The anecdote is hardly convincing as biography (an alternative tradition ascribes Epictetus' lameness to rheumatism), but it typifies a characteristic Stoic attitude. Epictetus' master, Epaphroditus, appears as a prominent character in Stages 33 and 34.

Some of Seneca's Stoic maxims might be presented to the class either in translation or in the original Latin, e.g. *magna servitus est magna fortuna*, 'great wealth is great slavery' (*ad Polybium de Consolatione* VI.5) and *qualis quisque sit, scies, si quemadmodum laudet, quemadmodum laudetur, aspexeris*', 'you can tell a man's character by noticing how he gives and receives praise' (*Epistulae Morales* LII.12). After guiding the class to the meaning of these maxims, invite pupils to say whether they agree with them.

On astrology, see the Unit IIA and IIB Handbook, pp. 68 and 73. Pliny, *Letters* II.20 describes a fraudulent use of astrology and *haruspicium* to wheedle a legacy from a dupe. Juvenal, *Satires* VI.565–91 colourfully denounces astrologers and their customers. Lewis and Reinhold II.409 has an example of an ancient horoscope. The reasons for astrology's perennial attraction might be discussed. What makes people look at newspaper horoscopes? Do the pupils look at horoscopes? Do they believe them?

Pupils might enjoy picking out the various signs of the zodiac which are clearly delineated on the relief shown on p. 82. The central roundel shows the slaying of the bull by Mithras. To the left and right stand Cautes and Cautopates: one with torch raised, symbolic of the Bull and the rising Sun, the other with torch pointing down, symbolic of the Scorpion and the setting Sun. The whole symbolised the struggle between the forces of good and evil, light and darkness, death and rebirth in nature.

The slaying of the bull is also shown in the drawing on p. 83 which is based on the reconstruction of the Carrawburgh Mithraeum in Newcastle Museum. In a cave-like building, the initiates recline on benches flanking the aisle.

Suggestions for further work

1 'Imagine that you are Euphrosyne and have returned to Chrysogonus in Athens. Describe to him your impressions of Rome.' Pupils should be encouraged to include things that might have impressed Euphrosyne favourably as well as unfavourably, and to refer to Stages 29–31 as well as 32 for material.

2 Read extracts from Petronius' *Cena Trimalchionis* in translation. The following sections all touch on topics dealt with or referred to in this stage: 32–3 extravagance at dinner; 34 wine; 35, 39 astrology; 47, 49 stuffed pig; 53 acrobats. See also the werewolf story in 62 and Trimalchio's instructions about his tomb in 71.

3 'Write a different lecture for Euphrosyne, keeping to her theme that Virtue matters more than Pleasure or Riches, but using a story or argument that would have a better chance of persuading Haterius and his friends than Euphrosyne's "poor man" story. If you wish, use the idea of a "rich man" story, as Euphrosyne intended to when she was interrupted.' Pupils will need plenty of help and preliminary discussion with this difficult exercise. The theme 'riches don't make you happy' could be developed by picturing the rich man, tormented by conscience, hated by those whom he exploits, befriended only by parasites and sycophants. Alternatively, the idea that 'you can't take your money with you when you die' could be explored; reference might be made to the custom of displaying a skeleton or similar *memento mori* at banquets (remind pupils of the skeleton mosaic in Stage 28, p. 141 and see Petronius *Cena* 34 and other references in Paoli 97), and to the parable of the rich fool in *Luke* 12.16–21).

Words and phrases checklist

The way in which *aequus* ('level') came to mean both 'calm' and 'right, fair' might be worth discussing.

STAGE 33: PANTOMĪMUS

Synopsis

Reading passages ⎱ ⎰Christianity
Background material ⎰ ⎱entertainment

Language notes   future and future perfect active

Title picture

This picture introduces the *pantomīmus* Paris and shows him with one of his masks. Note its closed mouth, which differentiates it from the types worn in other kinds of drama (compare, for example, the title picture for Stage 5).

Model sentences

Three forthcoming entertainments are announced: a performance by Paris in the theatre; chariot-races in the Circus; gladiatorial combats at the Colosseum.

The future tense is now introduced. The context, and the repeated *crās*, should be sufficient clues. Confirm the meaning of the new inflections if pupils ask about it; otherwise postpone comment until the story 'Tychicus' has been read.

The pictures and captions contain many opportunities to discuss details of the three types of entertainment described: the nature of Paris' performance; the dwarf Myropnous who accompanies him on the pipes; the central platform (*spīna*) round which the chariots in the Circus raced; the turning-posts (*mētae* – a word which pupils with long memories may recall from 'lūdī fūnebrēs' in Stage 15); the seven eggs, one of which was lowered at the end of each lap; the palm of victory; the keen interest and involvement of the emperor (Domitian's enthusiasm for chariot-racing was almost obsessive; later in his reign he established two *factiōnēs* of his own, purple and gold); the contest of *rētiāriī* and *murmillōnēs* in the Colosseum. More details of all three entertainments, especially *pantomīmī*, appear in the stories and background material.

The following words are new: *pantomīmus, tibiīs, duodecim, aurīgae*.

Tychicus

An outdoor performance by Paris at Haterius' villa (illustrated on p. 88), in front of Haterius' wife Vitellia and her friends, is interrupted by a fiery sermon from the Christian Tychicus, a client of Titus Flavius Clemens. Whereas Tychicus is fictitious, Clemens is historical. He was a cousin of Domitian and was put to death for 'atheism'; the accusation most probably refers to Judaism, conceivably to Christianity. Clemens will reappear in Stage 38.

It is worth noting that Tychicus' outburst is not directed at the content of Paris' performance but at the ecstatic, almost religious, adulation lavished upon Paris himself by the audience. The denunciations that pour from his lips may be contrasted with the story told by Euphrosyne in Stage 32 in which she propounds a frugal and disciplined quietism; the early Christians not only preached a gospel of peace but also proclaimed in fierce tones the imminent end of the world and the judgement to follow. Pupils might be asked, 'Which would be the more cheering message for those who led a poor and wretched life – Euphrosyne's sermon or Tychicus' prophecy?' This could be linked with the final sentence of the story which hints that Christianity found support especially among the less well-to-do and the downtrodden.

Tychicus' speech contains some echoes of the Vulgate, e.g. 1 *Thessalonians* 4.16–17.

Comprehension questions may be useful in dealing with the difficult last sentence of the first paragraph: 'Was Haterius there? Where had he gone? Why? What state was he in? Now translate the sentence.'

priusquam is used with the subjunctive in line 11. Encourage the class, by attention to the context, to prefer 'Before he could . . .' to 'Before he did . . .'

The future tense, introduced in the model sentences, is practised further in Tychicus' speech. *rēgnābit* (line 30) is pointedly contrasted with *nunc rēgnat* and anticipated by *in perpetuum*; Tychicus' next sentence begins with *mox*. The context, therefore, provides powerful clues to futurity. Once pupils appreciate that Tychicus' protest is leading naturally to threats about future judgement, they will easily recognise the meaning of the new forms of the verb.

Development of ablative usages continues in this stage, with the inclusion of the descriptive phrases *statūrā brevī* and *vultū sevērō* (lines 11–12).

The picture on p. 89 shows the 'chi-rho' monogram used by early Christians to refer to the name and person of Christ. It is composed of the first two letters of the Greek Χριστός ('Christ'), 'chi' (χ) and 'rho' (ρ).

in aulā Domitiānī

Paris was the most celebrated pantomimus of his day, and a favourite in
the imperial household (Juvenal, *Satires* VI.87 and VII.87–92). A
commemorative epigram by Martial (*Epigrams* XI.13) says that in Paris'
tomb lie

> *ars et gratia, lusus et voluptas,*
> *Romani decus et dolor theatri*
> *atque omnes Veneres Cupidinesque . . .*

He apparently came from Egypt and probably took the name Paris when
he became a pantomimus as it seems to have been a common stage-name.

Domitia, wife of Domitian, was the daughter of Nero's most successful
general, Cn. Domitius Corbulo. Domitian married her in A.D.70 and
when he succeeded to the principate in A.D.81 she was given the title
Augusta. Her affair with Paris is referred to by Suetonius, *Domitian* 3.

Myropnous, the dwarf, has been borrowed from the late second century
A.D. He appears on a Florentine tombstone of that date (see Bieber 236
and 305) playing the double pipes. The relief clearly shows his large
misshapen head and short, crippled legs (a drawing based on it appears in
Stage 40).

Epaphroditus (mentioned in passing in Stage 32 of the pupil's material,
also above, p. 134) was a freedman who became the secretary in charge of
petitions (*ā libellīs*), first of Nero and later of Domitian. He was one of the
group of powerful ministers who were in charge of important departments.

The language of the story is for the most part straightforward, and
pupils might work through Part I independently of the teacher, working
on their own or in pairs or groups, writing down the answers to the
printed comprehension questions. Subsequent class discussion might
include a comparison of the pupils' answers to question 7, which is more
wide-ranging and open-ended than the others. Paris' reactions to the
approach of Epaphroditus could be compared with those of Domitia;
some may feel that Paris cuts a more heroic figure than the agitated
Domitia, others that there is something irresponsible about his sang-froid.

The class might consider and comment on the nature of the roles acted
by Paris in this and the previous story: sensual, emotional, physical,
catering for mildly salacious or morbid tastes. For the love affair of Mars
and Venus, see Homer, *Odyssey* VIII.266ff., and for a description of its
enactment by a pantomimus, based on an account by Lucian, *De Saltatione*
63, see p. 99 of the pupil's material.

Other possible questions:

Why does Domitia come so near to tears (line 7)? Which part of the
story might provoke this response from her? Or is she responding to

the skill of the artist rather than anything in the story?
Why has Domitia asked Olympus to guard the door? Or, what
   evidence is there in lines 8–9 that Domitia is either nervous or guilty
   about Paris' performance?
Why does Paris describe Epaphroditus as *psittacum Domitiānī* (line 20)?

Pupils might also note the great power of Epaphroditus. Although he is
an ex-slave, he can frighten even the Emperor's wife through his hostility
and the activities of his spies.

The final sentence of Part I may cause difficulty; it can be tackled by
easy comprehension questions of the kind exemplified on p. 137 above and
on p. 30 of the Language Information pamphlet.

In Part II, alert pupils may spot Domitia's self-betrayal when she
answers Epaphroditus' inquiry about an unnamed pantomimus with a
mention of Paris. The question 'Why does Domitia go pale at
Epaphroditus' words in line 12?' will test whether the class is following the
story. They might discuss the significance of the coin placed on the lips as
Charon's fare (a picture of Charon and his boat appeared in Stage 22,
p. 41) and also the quasi-sepulchral style of Paris' final ridicule of
Epaphroditus. The formula *hīc iacet*, followed by three names, title, and
cause of death, is common (for simplification, *Augustī lībertus* has here been
placed after the cognomen, rather than in its more usual position after the
nomen). Part II is on the cassette.

The story provides plenty of opportunity for revising language points.
exstrūcta erat (I, line 1) can be compared with *exstruēbātur* and *exstrūcta est*,
and the reason for the feminine ending *exstrūcta* discussed. *cōnspicātī sumus*
(I, line 11) and *perscrūtātī estis* (II, line 12) provide practice of the 1st and
2nd persons of deponent verbs; *cōnspicātus sum, cōnspicātī erāmus, perscrūtātus
es* might be compared. Further practice of deponent verbs could be based
on the introductory notes to Part Two of the Language Information
pamphlet (p. 31).

First language note (future tense)

Encourage pupils to comment on the paradigms. In particular elicit that
the personal endings (-*ō* or -*m*, -*s*, -*t*, etc.) contain nothing that has not
been met already in other tenses; that the endings of the second
conjugation are easily recognised by analogy with the first, and those of
the fourth by analogy with the third (a point teachers can easily
demonstrate with such examples as *docēbunt, audiēmus*, etc.); that the 1st
person singular form of the third and fourth conjugation is something of
an 'odd man out'.

Further examples can readily be made up on the lines of paragraph 4,
nos. 6 and 7, e.g. *rogābimus, manēbunt, pugnābis, capiet, relinquētis, reveniam*.

Do not mix examples of the future with other tenses at this stage; pupils will need much more experience of the future before this can be a profitable exercise.

The paradigms in the pupil's text follow the convention that in written English 'shall' is used rather than 'will' in 1st-person forms if the context is one of futurity only and not volition. Whether and to what extent the pupils, too, should follow this convention is a matter for the teacher's discretion. But it would be undesirable to over-emphasise this detail at the expense of the main point of the language note, i.e. the new inflections and their significance.

Manipulation exercises and further practice

Exercise 1   Type: vocabulary
              Linguistic feature being practised: diminutives
The affectionate or contemptuous overtones of diminutives will be better understood when met in a poem or speech than in a word-list. Nevertheless, the point can be illustrated by teachers if they are prepared to supply a context. For instance, pupils may remember one of the previous occurrences of *homunculus*, as used for example by Eutychus to Clemens (Stage 18, 'in officīnā Eutychī', line 23) or by Modestus to Strythio (Stage 22, 'amor omnia vincit' II, line 27) or by Paris speaking of Epaphroditus in the present stage ('in aulā Domitiānī' I, line 28); the class could be asked 'Does it refer only to size or does it suggest anything else?' (If pupils stick, ask 'Does it suggest anything about the attitude of the speaker?') Similarly, overtones of endearment or affection can be illustrated from *filiolus*, as used by a mother speaking of her son.

libellus could be further discussed, in particular the development in its meaning from 'little book' to 'document' and so 'petition'; hence *ā libellīs*, 'secretary in charge of petitions', the official title of Epaphroditus. The connection between *libellus* and the English word 'libel' might also be demonstrated.

Exercise 2   Type: completion
              Missing item: participle
              Criterion of choice: sense
              Linguistic feature being practised: ablative absolute,
                  introduced in Stage 31
The blanks have to be filled not on the basis of morphology but by studying the situation described in the whole sentence; an incorrect choice will be either nonsensical or inappropriate in the context. The sentences offer plenty of scope for variety in translating the ablative absolute ('When the signal was given . . .', 'On the loss of his ship . . .', 'Turning their backs . . .', etc.).

Exercise 3   Type: transformation
                 Linguistic feature being practised: present and imperfect
                     passive, introduced in Stage 29

Some purely aural work at this point might provide a useful check on
pupils' ability to comprehend without translating, as well as giving them
practice in listening as opposed to reading. They could be asked to follow
by ear alone (i.e. without books), as the teacher reads a story from Unit
IIIA, such as 'in thermīs' (Stage 23), pausing from time to time to check,
by means of comprehension questions, that the story is being followed, or
asking the pupils to put their hands up every time a participle, or the
name of a person or place, is mentioned in a particular portion of text.
Similar practice could be based on the 'Longer Sentences' section of the
Unit IIIA Language Information pamphlet (pp. 26–7).

Second language note (future perfect tense)

The examples in paragraphs 1 and 4, though designed primarily to
introduce and practise the future perfect, also give further practice in the
simple future and provide incidental preparation for subsequent
discussion of conditional clauses. If pupils ask whether the future perfect
is used with any other introductory word than *sī*, they could be given an
example with *cum*, e.g. *cum ad urbem advēnerō, amīcum tuum vīsitābō*. This use
of *cum*, with reference to future time, could be contrasted with the familiar
use of *cum* with the subjunctive, where the reference is always to the past.

The background material

'Christianity' could appropriately be handled immediately after the story
'Tychicus' has been read; 'Entertainment' could be tackled at any point in
the stage.

Christianity

Pupils might consider why the Christians were unpopular and sometimes
persecuted. Discussion should focus not on the legal basis of persecutions
(a complex subject) but on the reasons for anti-Christian feeling. With a
little prompting, pupils may be able to produce such points as the
following:
   1   Most religions were able to co-exist happily with the official Roman
religion and even identify their own gods with Roman ones (as Sulis, for
example, was identified with Minerva), but such easy-going mutual
tolerance was quite unacceptable to the monotheistic Jews and Christians.
The Christians' failure to worship the Roman gods made them unpopular,

since it was widely believed that failure to sacrifice could provoke the gods to punish the community; St Augustine (*De Civitate Dei* II.3) quotes a proverb: 'no rain, because of Christians'. This may be part of the reason why Christians were regarded as anti-social and even misanthropic. (Tacitus, *Annals* XV.44 speaks of their *odium generis humani*.) Refusal to worship the Roman gods was not in itself a criminal offence, but it could be used as evidence that an accused person was a Christian, as Pliny's letter to Trajan (*Letters* X.96) shows.

2   Misinterpretation of such phrases in the Christian liturgy as 'Love one another' and 'This is my body . . . take and eat . . .' gave rise to lurid suspicions of sexual orgies, incest, infanticide and cannibalism.

3   The Roman authorities were generally suspicious of anything that looked like a secret society, fearing political subversion. This anxiety, often focusing on *collēgia*, is evident on several occasions in the Pliny-Trajan correspondence, most strikingly perhaps in *Letters* X.34, where such apprehensions lead Trajan to veto the formation of a fire-brigade.

4   The peace was often disturbed by confrontations between Jews and Christians. *Acts* 21 has a lively account of a fracas of this kind. Suetonius' reference (*Claudius* 25) to Jews *impulsore Chresto assidue tumultuantes* may be a reference to other such incidents.

Nero's persecution of the Christians is described by Tacitus, *Annals* XV.44; the quotation from Trajan in the pupil's text is part of the famous exchange between Pliny and Trajan (Pliny, *Letters* X.96 and 97). These texts might be studied in translation by the class. St Paul's reference to the *domus Caesaris*, mentioned at the top of p. 98 of the pupil's text, is in *Philippians* 4.22. C.S.C.P. *Roman World* Unit I, Book 1, *Lugdunum*, includes a description of the second-century persecution at Lyons, and other contemporary material abusing and defending Christians.

The narrative in the pupil's text could be continued with a mention of later developments in Rome's relations with Christianity. By the Edict of Toleration (311) and the Edict of Milan (313), Christianity became a legal and officially tolerated religion. The first Christian emperor was Constantine (sole emperor 324–37), who nevertheless continued to support and participate in the official state religion as well; for example, his new city Constantinople was consecrated with both Roman and Christian rites. Christianity became the official religion of the empire under Theodosius (379–95).

The Hinton St Mary mosaic, the central roundel of which is shown on p. 98, has now been relaid on the landing in front of the Roman Britain gallery in the British Museum. It dates from the fourth century A.D. This bust is almost certainly intended to represent Christ, with the 'chi-rho' (see p. 137) above) behind him and pomegranates, symbols of immortality, on either side.

Entertainment

The Theatre of Pompey, shown on p. 100, stood in the Campus Martius. It was built by Pompey the Great in 55 B.C. The building behind it is an *ōdēum*, or concert-hall.

Pantomime. For good detailed accounts, see Balsdon, *Life* 274ff. and Bieber 165–6, 227, 235–7. The word *pantomīmus* is used both of the dancer and of his dance. The orchestra accompanying him varied from small to huge; instruments included the double pipes (as played by Myropnous in the stories), lyre, trumpets and *scabella* (wooden clappers operated by the foot). According to Lucian, *De Saltatione* 61, who wrote in the Antonine period and is our chief source on pantomimi, the dancer was required to know the whole of Homer, Hesiod and the Greek tragedies. Lucian defends the art vigorously against criticisms of immorality and bad taste: 'It exercises the body and sharpens the wits; it delights and instructs the spectator with stories from the past, charming his eyes and ears with pipes and cymbals and graceful movement . . . it improves the moral character,· too, by filling the audience with indignation at the deeds of the villain and pity for the sufferings of the victim' (*De Saltatione* 72). The degree of detail expected of a pantomimus' gestures, and the way in which strict conventions controlled the performance, are well illustrated by the anecdote of the unfortunate pantomimus who muddled the two sets of gestures for 'Cronos devouring his children' and 'Thyestes devouring his children' (Lucian, *De Saltatione* 80).

Chariot-racing. Balsdon, *Life* 314–24 gives a full and entertaining account, with a rich fund of anecdote from which a selection could be retold to pupils. For a *dēfixiō* cursing charioteers and horses, see Stage 22, p. 41 and the commentary on p. 22 above. Pliny's criticisms of chariot-racing (*Letters* IX.6) could usefully be read and discussed, in particular his claims that the racing is essentially repetitive and that the spectators are less interested in the speed of the horses and the skill of the charioteers than in seeing their own team win. Ovid has a light-hearted description of watching the races with a female companion in *Amores* III.2, translated in C.S.C.P. *The Roman World* Unit II, item 14. An inscription commemorating the great charioteer Diocles (*I.L.S.* 5287, also *C.I.L.* VI. 10048) is translated in Dudley 214–5 (but with wrong reference) and in Lewis and Reinhold II.230–2.

The questions on the chariot-racing relief on p. 101 are examples of the kinds that could be asked about many of the pictures. Pupils may need to be reminded that such visual evidence is an important part of our knowledge of the Roman world. Encourage them to pick out details, like the reins tied tightly round the charioteer's body, and connect them with other information they have. Question 2 may cause difficulty. The conical pillars mark the turning-point (*mēta*) at the end of the central platform (*spīna*) and were tall (about 4.75 m, 16 ft) so that the charioteers could gauge their distance from the turn. The egg-shaped pinnacles on top are not the eggs that marked the number of laps completed but part of the pillars. The inscription reads ANNIAE ARESCVSA but its significance is not known. The relief dates from the first century A.D. and is in the British Museum.

Gladiatorial combats. Pupils will doubtless remember much of the material in Stage 8. The gladiatorial salutation to the emperor, '*moritūrī tē salūtant*', can be linked with the language note on the future participle in Stage 32.

Carcopino 256ff. has a detailed acount of the Colosseum. The photograph of the interior on p. 102 of the pupil's text shows the cells in which the prisoners and animals were kept under the floor of the arena, and some of the internal structure that supported the rows of seats.

Dinner entertainment. Balsdon, *Life* 44–9 and Paoli 98 are helpful. Some of the following source material could be used: Pliny, *Letters* IX.17 (cultured and coarse entertainment; Pliny is more tolerant towards the latter than might have been expected); Petronius, *Cena* 53 (acrobats); Pliny, *Letters* V.19 (the versatile entertainer Zosimus); Martial, *Epigrams* XI.52.16–18 (a host promises not to recite even if his guest does); Pliny, *Letters* III.5.11–12 (Pliny's uncle objects to an interruption at a reading); Juvenal, *Satires* XI.162–4 (Spanish dancing-girls); Horace, *Satires* II.8 (an extravagant meal); Pliny, *Letters* VII.24 (Ummidia Quadratilla); Horace, *Satires* I.5.50–70 (a slanging-match between two clowns).

Suggestions for further work

1 It would be educationally valuable to link pupils' study of Christianity here with any work on early Christian history which they might have done in R.E. lessons. The narrative of St Paul's journeys in *Acts of the Apostles* can be explored for references to Roman law, government and religion. In chapter 18, for example, the governor of Achaea, Seneca's brother Gallio, refuses to get involved in a Jewish-Christian dispute; in chapter 19, the silversmiths who sell souvenir models of the great temple of Diana at Ephesus protest vigorously against Paul's preachings; in chapter 22, Paul lays claim to Roman citizenship, somewhat to the amazement of the Roman officer in charge, who has obtained his own citizenship only through bribery; in chapter 25, Paul appeals as a Roman citizen to Caesar against a sentence of flogging.

2 Stoic and Christian attitudes to slavery could be compared by looking at Seneca, *Epistulae Morales* 47 and Paul's letter to Philemon.

3   Younger pupils may be interested in some of the cryptograms used as signs and passwords by early Christians, such as the ROTAS-OPERA-TENET-AREPO-SATOR word-square (details in Ellis, also quoted in Widdess 90).

4   'Write a description of a chariot-race, perhaps in the form of a running commentary on the race as it takes place.' This may prove a suitable exercise for tape-recording. Some ideas for incidents could be supplied from the Sidonius Apollinaris story described in Balsdon, *Life* 317; and afterwards teachers might read their classes the chariot-race narrative from Sophocles, *Electra* 698–763.

STAGE 34: LĪBERTUS

Synopsis

Reading passages   the freedman Epaphroditus

Background material   freedmen

Language notes   present passive infinitive
                               3rd person singular and plural, future passive

---

Title picture

This shows Epaphroditus in his toga, which he became entitled to wear when he was freed. On the table behind is his *pilleus*, the felt cap received by freedmen and freedwomen at manumission and worn on ceremonial occasions.

ultiō Epaphrodītī

Epaphroditus seeks revenge for his humiliation in the previous stage. He has the support of the jealous Emperor, suspicious of the relationship between Domitia and Paris. But in spite of Domitia's earlier fears, Epaphroditus cannot move openly. Salvius, reappearing after absence in Britain, undertakes to concoct a suitable plan.

In this stage, as in Stage 33, Epaphroditus appears as a figure of great power and influence. His network of spies and agents (*ministrī*) was mentioned in Stage 33 (p. 90); in the present stage he is able to call on the obedient services of the praetorian guard. Such power, wielded by an ex-slave, may surprise pupils. But though the events of Stage 34 are fiction, there is plenty of historical evidence for the power of imperial freedmen. For example, in the crisis caused by the activities of Claudius' wife Messalina in A.D.48, when Claudius was helpless, his freedman Narcissus took the responsibility for ordering Messalina's death (Tacitus, *Annals* XI.37); and his three chief freedmen sponsored the rival candidates for the position of Claudius' next wife (XII.1ff.).

The 3rd person form of the future passive is introduced in this story. Pupils should normally be able to cope successfully, probably without realising that it is new. The context should help, and the new form is a combination of two elements which they have already met: the future active, met in Stage 33, and the 3rd person passive ending *-ur*, met in Stage 29.

īnsidiae

Domitian's suspicions about Paris' and Domitia's relationship, followed by Paris' death in A.D.83 and a divorce between Domitian and Domitia, are historical (Suetonius, *Domitian* 3; Dio Cassius, *Roman History* LXVII.3); the circumstances in the pupil's text are invention.

Most of the printed questions are straightforward and could be tackled by pupils working on their own during their first reading of the passage (see p. 138 above, on 'in aulā Domitiānī'). Further questions could be added as appropriate, e.g. 'Why did Domitia pause on the threshold of Vitellia's room?' Later discussion might follow up question 5 by considering whether Domitia's explanation is probable, or even possible. Use question 9 to establish that Salvius' plan is not primarily a murder plot, but a 'frame-up', as already foreshadowed in lines 10–12 of 'ultiō Epaphrodītī': Paris and Domitia are to be caught together in suspicious circumstances. Paris' earlier enactment of the discovered love affair of Mars and Venus is to be performed again, this time unwittingly and in grim earnest.

Pupils might be asked 'What mood or atmosphere is built up in lines 24–8?' If they are asked 'Which words contribute to this mood?' they should be able to point to such words and phrases as *dēsertam* (line 24), *obscūrum* (line 26) and *in silentiō* (line 27). Suspense and menace are also built up through the presentation of the central character (Domitiā) at first in a group, then with only one companion, and finally alone. Such effects are employed with great skill by Tacitus, for example in *Annals* XIV.8 (Agrippina) and *Histories* III.84 (Vitellius), and by such film directors as Alfred Hitchcock, for example in *Psycho*.

The story contains two examples of the present infinitive passive, and two deponent infinitives. (One example of a deponent infinitive, *ulcīscī*, has already appeared in the previous story, line 1.) In each case, let the

context establish the sense; for example, *parārī* (line 6) is anticipated by
parāre (line 5). Confirm, if necessary, that the *-ī* ending is an infinitive;
pupils may well have noted the deponent infinitive already in the
introduction of Part Two of the Language Information pamphlet (p. 31).
Further discussion should normally be postponed until the language note
is read.

The story is suitable for work on participles. Pupils could be asked to
pick them out and say what case or number or gender they are, or what
noun they agree with, whether they are present, perfect active or perfect
passive, or whether they are being used with *est*, etc. to form a perfect
tense.

Encourage idiomatic translation of the sentences involving *dum* (line
28) and *priusquam* (lines 33–4) with the subjunctive. (One example of
priusquam appeared in Stage 33, 'Tychicus', line 11.) Sentences involving
priusquam and *dum* are included in the 'Uses of the subjunctive' section of
the Language Information pamphlet (p. 29).

This story is on the cassette.

exitium

Pace is essential for reading this story. Some of the easier sections could be
covered by comprehension questions alone (after an initial reading aloud
by the teacher) without a formal translation. Afterwards, class and
teacher can return to selected lines or sections for a more leisurely
consideration of character (Myropnous, Domitia, Paris), historical details
(e.g. the praetorian guard) or linguistic features (e.g. ablative absolute
phrases).

Ensure that pupils realise that in the drawing on p. 111 Paris is posing
behind the statue in order to hide from the praetorian guard (see line 9). A
blackboard plan of the house on the lines of the diagram in Stage 1, p. 13
and showing *iānua, ātrium, triclīnium, culīna, cubicula, hortus, postīcum* and
faucēs (passage from *iānua* to *ātrium*) may also help them to visualise the
sequence of events.

This story is on the cassette.

Some suggested questions on Part II

What unpleasant discovery did Paris and Domitia make at the back
door?
Why did Paris dart out before dashing back into the garden?
Where did he hide?
What noise did Paris hear?
Where did Paris leap from? Where to? Why did he miss his footing?

Paris' agility in lines 18–20, already evident in Stage 33, 'in aulā Domitiānī' I, line 29, where he climbs quickly up a pillar, is a reminder that his profession as a pantomimus called for physical strength and skill as well as artistic talent.

The long sentence *intereā Domitia . . . venīret* (lines 23–4) could initially be approached by easy comprehension questions of the kind suggested on p. 137 above and on p. 30 of the pupil's Language Information pamphlet.

ingredientur (I, line 6) is the first example of a deponent verb in the future tense. Its meaning should be readily inferred from the context. There are more examples in the next story.

First language note (present passive infinitive)

Invite comments on paragraph 3, and if pupils do not themselves raise the question of the form of the third conjugation, ask them which passive infinitive differs from the others.

Paragraph 5 deals with the deponent infinitive; comparison with paragraph 3 can be used to demonstrate the essential nature of the deponent verb. Ask, for example, 'In what way is the deponent infinitive like a passive infinitive? In what way is it like an active one?' Discussion like this puts the rather abstract statement that 'deponent verbs are passive in form but active in meaning' into more intelligible terms.

honōrēs

In return for his services, Salvius is promised the consulship, and his career reaches a new peak. He did in fact hold the office, some time before A.D.86. Epaphroditus is promised the *ōrnāmenta praetōria* (described in the pupil's text, p. 123). Myropnous, overhearing their conversation and learning of Salvius' responsibility for Paris' death, vows revenge.

After divorcing Domitia, Domitian took his niece Julia (widow of the consul Sabinus who appeared in Stage 32) into the palace as his mistress. In A.D.84, however, Domitia was restored and both she and Julia lived together with Domitian. Domitia was probably privy to the successful conspiracy in A.D.96 against Domitian's life.

Epaphroditus was put to death on Domitian's orders in A.D.95.

Pupils have already met two examples of a noun and participle in the dative case placed at the front of the sentence (*praecōnī regressō*, Stage 31, 'salūtātiō' II, lines 4–5; *Hateriō hoc rogantī*, Stage 32, 'philosophia', line 38). Note how they cope with the example *Salviō aulam intrantī* in line 1 here.

comitābitur (line 10) can be used to demonstrate to pupils that the context often makes it plain whether a particular verb is passive or deponent. The class could be told 'there is a deponent verb *comitārī* and

also an ordinary verb *comitāre*, both meaning "accompany". But it is clear
from the sentence that *comitābitur* here means "will accompany", not
"will be accompanied". Why?'

The word order *ē latebrīs rēpsit Myropnous* (lines 18–19) might be
discussed, and attempts made to reproduce it in English.

pereat in the final line anticipates the introduction of the present
subjunctive in Stage 36.

The consular symbols in the drawing on p. 114 are based on those
shown on a series of coins issued by the consuls in the last years of the
Republic. The *fascēs*, a bundle of rods tied with a red thong, was carried
before a senior magistrate by a lictor. A consul had twelve lictors. The axe
in each bundle was carried only outside Rome. The folding ivory *sella
curūlis* was the chair of office on which a senior magistrate sat when
conducting official business.

Second language note (3rd person singular and plural, future passive)

As noted above (p. 146), the introduction of the future passive into the
linguistic scheme develops naturally out of previous work and should
cause little or no difficulty. Comparison between the passive forms
(paragraph 2) and the deponents (paragraph 4) can be used to re-
emphasise the point that the deponent verbs are exactly like the passive of
ordinary verbs in form, differing from them only in meaning.

Manipulation exercises

Exercise 1   Type: vocabulary
              Linguistic feature being practised: nouns in *-ātiō*
This exercise can be used to exemplify the point that a Latin word
normally has several different English translations. Thus, pupils might
translate *coniūrātiō* either as 'conspiracy' (by analogy with 'conspire' in the
adjacent column) or as 'plot' (from recollection of its use in Stage 13, etc.):
salūtātiō may produce the general term 'greeting' (by analogy with the
familiar *salūtāre*), or the specific term 'morning visit' (remembered from
Stage 31). Encourage this flexibility; it will be crucial when pupils reach
original Latin literature.

Exercise 2   Type: completion
              Missing item: verb
              Criterion of choice: morphology
              Linguistic feature being practised: future tense, introduced in
                  Stage 33

Exercise 3   Type: translation from English, using restricted pool of
                 Latin words
             Linguistic features being practised: imperfect passive,
                 indirect command, perfect passive participle, relative
                 pronouns, ablative absolute

Exercise 4   Type: transformation
             Linguistic feature being practised: perfect and pluperfect
                 passive, introduced in Stage 30

This exercise is similar to Stage 33 exercise 3, but is more difficult, as
it requires the manipulation of the pluperfect and perfect tenses.
A 1st-person example is included in sentences 5a and 5b.

The background material

There is much helpful information on freedmen and freedwomen in Crook
(especially 50–55) and Duff, and the number of relevant references in
Latin inscriptions and literature is immense. A selection from the
following material could be used with pupils, some points being elicited
from the class in discussion, others being presented by teachers, and
others ferreted out by the pupils' researches. Care needs to be taken over
the quantity of information presented to the class; the right amount of
detail can illustrate the information in the pupil's text in a lively and
interesting way, but too much will lead to confusion. The following sub-
headings roughly follow the order in which the information is presented in
the pupil's text:

Definition of freedmen. It may be necessary to remind pupils of the difference
between a freeborn man (*ingenuus*) and a freedman (*lībertus*). Both are free
(*līberī*), but the *ingenuus* has always been so, whereas the *lībertus* has
previously been a slave.

Legal status of freedmen. The legal status granted to ex-slaves was noticeably
more generous in ancient Rome than in other slave-owning societies, such
as classical Athens or the southern states of the U.S.A. in the nineteenth
century, inasmuch as the freedman of a Roman citizen became a Roman
citizen himself, and although his citizen rights were subject to the
limitations described in the pupil's text, the limitations were relatively few
and the freedman's children were wholly exempt from them.

Motives for manumission. These might be financial (see pupil's text, p. 120)
or humanitarian. A slave might also be manumitted as a reward for long
service or for some exceptional action; pupils have met some relevant
details in Stage 6, p. 14.

Obligations to ex-master. The technical term for the work performed by a freedman for his ex-master was *operae*; the number of days on which *operae* were to be performed was normally specified at the time of manumission. Strictly speaking, the *operae* of a freedman had to be of the same kind as he had performed while a slave and were to be performed only for the ex-master; Crook (52 and 192) notes some entertaining exceptions to this rule. *'operae'* came to mean not only 'work' but 'workers' (often 'hired workers', hence the meaning 'hired thugs' which the pupils met in Stage 18).

A proposal that ex-masters should have the power to re-enslave undutiful freedmen was strongly supported in the Senate but rejected by Nero (Tacitus, *Annals* XIII.26–7).

Prejudice against freedmen. Dionysius of Halicarnassus (*Roman Antiquities* IV.24. 4–8, quoted in Lewis and Reinhold II.53) is indignant and abusive about freedmen; Persius (*Satires* V.78ff., quoted by Crook 50) is sour and sarcastic. Some of the material referred to above (p. 125) in connection with 'graded dinner-parties' indicates the readiness of some masters to humiliate their freedmen. Horace (*Satires* I.6) defends himself vigorously against those who sneered at him for being a freedman's son.

Opportunities for freedmen. It has been said that freedmen were 'probably the most intelligent class of the community' (Buckland and McNair, 186). Crook (50) points out that this generalisation underestimates the range of class covered, but he adds: 'nevertheless, the freedman class certainly did include many people of high intelligence, literacy, energy and ambition'. Perhaps those freedmen who came off least well at manumission were those whose 'assets' in the labour market had declined with the years – for example, those who had originally been purchased for the sake of their muscle-power or physical beauty.

Freedmen's sons who achieved high status. These include Horace, the Emperor Pertinax, and the brutal ex-praetor Larcius Macedo (Pliny, *Letters* III.14).

The relief shown on p. 120 comes from Mariemont, Belgium. A lictor is touching the kneeling slave with a rod (*vindicta*). A slave already freed (on the left) is shaking hands with a fourth person, probably his master. Both slaves are wearing the *pilleus*.

Interpreting the inscriptions in the pupil's text may best be done by teacher and class working together. The translations are as follows:

1 In memory of Titus Flavius Homerus, a generous ex-master, Titus Flavius Hyacinthus (erected this tomb).   *C.I.L.* VI.18109

2. In memory of Julius Vitalis, a well-deserving freedman, his ex-master (erected this tomb).

3 Titus Flavius Eumolpus and Flavia Quinta built (this tomb) for themselves, their freedmen and freedwomen and their descendants.

C.I.L. VI.18052

4 Titus Flavius Cerialis erected (this tomb) in memory of Flavia Philaenis
   his freedwoman and wife who served him well.
                                                      C.I.L. VI.18017

Notice the abbreviations:

D.M.	*dīs mānibus*	'to the spirits of the departed'
B.M.	*bene merentī*	a conventional phrase meaning 'who was a good man' or 'who deserved this kindness'
B.M.F.	*bene merentī fēcit*	

Imperial freedmen. These followed the normal rule of taking their ex-master's praenomen and nomen on manumission. Thus Epaphroditus, on being manumitted by Nero, would be known in full as 'Tiberius Claudius, Neronis Augusti libertus, Epaphroditus'. A simplified version of this name and title is used in the pupil's text, Stage 33, p. 93.

The more power was concentrated in the hands of the emperor, the greater became the influence of the emperor's personal entourage. Augustus had used his slaves and freedmen as secretaries and clerks; Claudius went further by developing a 'civil service', in which the various departments were headed by freedmen. In addition to the secretaries mentioned in the pupil's text, there were also secretaries *ā cognitiōnibus* (responsible for administration of judicial inquiries) and *ā studīs* (libraries and literary advice). The power of such men reached its peak under Claudius and Nero.

Pliny's indignant letters about Pallas are *Letters* VII.29, VIII.6. The senatorial debate about the grant of *ōrnāmenta praetōria* to Pallas is described in Tacitus, *Annals* XII.53. Crook (63) points out that the great fortunes of men like Pallas and Narcissus were subject to the rule that on a freedman's death his ex-master (in this case, the emperor) was entitled to a proportion of his property.

Imperial freedmen are often at the centre of dramatic episodes in first-century Roman history. For example, the freedman Narcissus was sent to quell the mutiny of the army at Boulogne on the eve of the invasion of Britain in A.D.43. According to Dio (*Roman History* LX.19), the soldiers' rebelliousness dissolved into mirth at the sight of an ex-slave giving orders from the general's tribunal; they greeted him with shouts of '*iō Saturnālia!*', a reference to the festival at which slaves dressed up in their masters' . clothes. For the roles played by Claudius' freedmen at and after the death of Messalina, see p. 146 above. Tacitus (*Annals* XIV.3–8) gives a vivid picture of the freedman Anicetus' involvement in the murder of Agrippina. A less dramatic, but remarkably long, career was enjoyed by the imperial freedman (name unknown; his son was called Claudius Etruscus), born in Smyrna about 3 A.D., who served continuously under ten successive emperors, from Tiberius to Domitian, except for a brief period of exile in his old age and died in A.D.92 (Statius, *Silvae* III.3).

Words and phrases checklist

In the second part of this checklist, a number of common deponent verbs are gathered together. Pupils might first be asked to translate the three forms given for a particular verb, e.g. *cōnor, cōnārī, cōnātus sum*; then teachers might pick out for translation some assorted examples from the forms given in the list, e.g. *sequī, hortātus sum, profectus sum, adipīscor*; finally other inflections could be practised, e.g. *loquēbantur, ingressī erant, cōnspicāta est.*

The Language Information pamphlet

About the language

The sub-sections dealing with nouns, adjectives and pronouns have now, with the inclusion of the ablative, virtually reached their final form, in which they will appear in all subsequent Language Information pamphlets of this course. The sub-sections dealing with verbs, and with some syntactic points, now contain most of the commonest inflections and constructions but have still to be expanded in later Units by the addition of various passive and subjunctive forms, and such constructions as indirect statement.

Nouns (pp. 4–5). Paragraph 4 seeks to show, by practical demonstration rather than abstract statement, that the stem from which the oblique cases of 3rd declension nouns are formed does not necessarily appear in the nominative singular. When the pupils have produced *duce*, *ducibus*, etc., it may be useful to practise the words in context, e.g. *mīlitēs, ā duce laudātī* ... or *servī, itinere dēfessī* ..., etc., thus reminding the class of the function of the ablative and not leaving the examples as isolated words.

A similar exercise can of course be carried out with other cases. In particular, an instruction to produce the accusative singular and plural of assorted 3rd declension nouns (e.g. *flōs, iter, legiō, flūmen*) might provide helpful revision of the difference in formation between neuter and other nouns.

For a suggested exercise on 4th declension nouns, see p. 131 above.

Adjectives (pp. 6–7). Paragraph 4 gives practice in handling nouns and adjectives in the same case but of different declensions. The two instances where an ablative is required have been indicated. After the examples have been worked, the class might be asked why the required case is ablative; some will remember the note on prepositions in Stage 28 and perhaps recall which particular preposition would be used here. The exercise can be extended for further oral work, using nouns and adjectives on pp. 4–6 of the pupil's text, e.g. to practise 4th and 5th declension nouns, though some of the noun + adjective combinations ('huge knees', etc.) will be faintly bizarre. If pupils ask about word order, confirm that noun + adjective is commoner than adjective + noun, but this point should not be allowed to distract attention from the main topic under consideration, i.e. the inflections.

Comparison of adjectives (pp. 8–9). After paragraphs 3 and 4 have

been studied, comment might be invited not only on the neuter forms
mentioned in paragraph 4 but also on the ablative singular of the
comparative; pupils could be asked to contrast the ablative of *longior* first
with 3rd declension nouns such as *mercātor* and *tempus*, then with the
adjectives *fortis* and *ingēns*, and to say what they notice. Invite comment on
the forms of *longissimus* to elicit its similarity with *bonus*.

Pronouns (pp. 10–13). If asked to comment on *īdem* (paragraph 7) and
its relationship with *is* (paragraph 6), pupils will probably say that *īdem*
consists of the various forms of *is*, with -*dem* on the end. Confirm this, and
encourage further comment. When they spot the exceptions to the rule
(*eundem, eōrundem*, etc.) invite them to suggest reasons why these forms
should have been used rather than the non-existent *eumdem, eōrumdem*, etc.
Discussion of this kind may help to pave the way for some aspects of
compound verbs which pupils will meet later, e.g. the combination of *cum*
+ *dō* to produce *condō, cum* + *dūcō* to produce *condūcō*, etc.

Verbs (pp. 14–19). Some pupils may be disheartened by the quantity
of verb morphology on these pages. In providing reassurance, the teacher
may find it helpful to make some of the following points:

1 Some parts of the verb are met much oftener than others; most of the
   forms that occur most frequently are already familiar to pupils (present,
   imperfect, perfect and pluperfect indicative active, imperfect and
   pluperfect subjunctive active).
2 The 'personal' endings of the verb's active forms vary very little from
   tense to tense. This can be exemplified by putting a present subjunctive
   such as *audiāmus* on the board, and demonstrating to the class that
   although it is a part of the verb they have never seen before, they know,
   without being told, whether it refers to 'I', 'you', 'he', 'we' or 'they'.
3 The context of the sentence often makes the significance of the verb-
   ending obvious. The present subjunctive can again be used as an
   illustration. Put *in hōc theātrō adsumus ut fābulam spectēmus* on the board, to
   demonstrate that anyone who can cope with the first four words will
   also get the rest of the sentence right, including the unfamiliar form
   spectēmus.

In a reading course, as opposed to a composition course, there is no great
virtue in requiring pupils to learn paradigms by heart; what matters is
that they should be able to recognise the inflections and translate them
correctly in their reading, or (if stuck) be able to find their way around the
paradigms in a work of reference like the Language Information
pamphlet. But some pupils, still anxious perhaps about the large number
of verb inflections, may ask to be allowed to learn them. Explain that
recognition matters more than memorisation and stress the importance of
being able to *translate* an inflection, not just recite it in a paradigm; also
point out that not all tenses are of equal importance, so that there is much

more point in learning (say) the imperfect than the future perfect. But it would be merely doctrinaire to *forbid* them to learn paradigms. The pupils' belief that memorisation of the paradigms will help them with their reading can sometimes be a self-fulfilling prophecy.

Indicative active (pp. 14–15). The problem posed by the similarity between the 2nd conjugation's present tense and the 3rd and 4th conjugation's future tense should not be explored until pupils have securely grasped the general principles behind the future tense's formation. For most pupils, this will mean the problem should be postponed until Unit IVA.

The exercise in paragraph 4 is demanding, and is intended primarily for oral work. If attempted as individual written work (and this is only recommended for very able pupils), the following points should be borne in mind. Since the object of this and similar exercises is to reinforce understanding of the paradigm the class should be discouraged from attempting the exercise from memory without referring to the paradigm; if ambitious pupils want to attempt the exercise from memory alone, insist that they check their answers from the paradigm afterwards. On the importance of working through such exercises word by word, see above, pp. 72–3.

Indicative passive (pp. 16–17). In paragraph 2, as a reminder that the 3rd person singular can be translated by 'she' or 'it', invite pupils to improve on *'he* is being destroyed' for *dēlētur*, and practise similar variations with other examples. The teacher should be guided by the experience and confidence of the class in tackling paragraphs 5 and 6. If pupils are very competent, or have reached a late stage of Unit IIIB, the paragraphs can be covered quite quickly as oral work round the class. But if pupils are tentative, then give them plenty of time; let them discuss the examples among themselves in pairs or groups, and postpone if necessary the two examples in paragraph 6 ('he was carried' and 'they were heard') which practise the more difficult mode of translating the perfect passive. The examples in paragraph 7 should be translated and discussed. Further practice involving non-masculine forms of the participle could include some 3rd person singular examples where no subject is expressed and 'she' or 'it' has to be supplied (e.g. *laudāta est, dēlētum est*, etc.) and end with a discussion of one or two examples of other persons (e.g. *iussa sum, ductae sunt*, etc.) where English lacks a differentiating pronoun.

If, in the later stages of reading a Unit, pupils are having problems with a particular item of morphology, such as one of the passive tenses, it is occasionally helpful for them to go back and re-do an exercise from the Language Information pamphlet that has been worked some time before. Insecure pupils can find this a very effective type of remedial work, but it should be employed sparingly because of the danger of boredom.

Other forms (pp. 18–19). Pupils should compare the paradigm of the present participle in paragraph 3 with that of *ingēns* on p. 6; the participles and gerundives in paragraphs 4–6 can be compared with *bonus*.

In the absence of a natural English equivalent to the Latin gerundive, the latter is here translated not in isolation, but in the context of complete sentences. If pupils ask such questions as 'What does *portandus* mean on its own?', perhaps the least unsatisfactory answer is 'having to be carried'. Although such an answer has drawbacks, especially when applied to impersonal uses such as *currendum est*, it goes some way towards explaining the presence of *est* in *amphora portanda est*, and the agreement between *amphora* and *portanda*. Some gerundives that have found their way into English might be quoted and explained, e.g. addenda, agenda, corrigenda and the names Amanda and Miranda. Further practice of gerundives might include sentences where the agent is not expressed, e.g. *urbs dēlenda est*. Pupils have met one example of this sentence pattern (*Haterius ... laudandus est*) in Stage 32, 'philosophia', line 23.

Deponent verbs (pp. 20–1). This section is more advanced and more demanding than the language note on deponent verbs in Stage 32; 1st and 2nd person forms have been included in the perfect and pluperfect tenses, and the practice in paragraphs 3 and 4 presupposes considerable familiarity with deponents. For easier practice of deponent verbs in this Language Information pamphlet, see p. 159 below, on the introduction to the 'Words and phrases' section.

When pupils tackle paragraph 5, ask them to find specific correspondences between the passive forms of *portō* and *trahō* and the forms of the two deponent verbs in paragraph 1 (e.g. *cōnātur – portātur; locūtī erant – tractī erant*) and encourage comment both on the similarity of form and on the extent of the difference in meaning e.g. ' *-bantur* always indicates "they" and is always imperfect; but if the verb is deponent it means "they" were doing something, and if the verb is an ordinary one it means "they" were having something done to them.' It is important that comment of this kind should come from the pupils, not from the teacher. Deponent verbs, though usually easy to cope with in reading, are often tricky to discuss; comment from teachers will be confusing if pupils have not already grasped the point for themselves, and superfluous if they have.

Pupils' earlier experience of participles can be used to reinforce the comparison between ordinary and deponent verbs. Thus, the following examples might be put up on the board:

parābātur he was being prepared	*cōnābātur* he was trying
parātus erat he had been prepared	*cōnātus erat* he had tried etc.

After these examples have been discussed and their meanings compared, the class could look again at the distinction drawn in Stages 21 and 22:

parātus   *cōnātus*

having been prepared   having tried   etc.

Pupils may be able to see for themselves how the difference between the participles fits into a general pattern of difference between ordinary and deponent verbs.

Anxious pupils may ask 'How can I tell whether an ending like *-bantur* is passive or deponent?' On the whole, the later they raise this question, the more fully it can be answered, since an answer at a later stage can make use of the pupils' increased experience of, and familiarity with, deponents. Teachers could demonstrate that the sentence as a whole normally gives clues to the nature of the verb (pupils might be asked to compare *puella ē domō ēgrediēbātur* and *servus ad rēgem dūcēbātur*), that the 'Words and phrases' section of the Language Information pamphlet will always supply an answer, and that pupils already know from experience whether some verbs are deponent or not (e.g. they can all handle *ingressus est* correctly through familiarity with the active participle *ingressus*).

Irregular Verbs (pp. 22–4). If pupils ask, confirm that there is no passive of *esse, posse, velle* or (except for some isolated forms) *īre*.

These verbs provide a convenient opportunity for the class to practise handling the various technical terms ('3rd person', 'plural', 'pluperfect', etc.). Ask pupils to describe assorted examples (*capiam, fert, ībant, fēcī, vellēmus*, etc.) in the way described in Unit IIB Language Information pamphlet, p. 16. A translation should be required at the same time, and the labels 'indicative' and 'subjunctive' could be added if pupils have a good grasp of them.

On the rather difficult exercise in paragraph 3, see the comments above (p. 156) on the similar exercise in paragraph 4 of 'Verbs: Indicative active'.

Uses of the cases (pp. 24–5). This section is intended primarily for pupils to refer to during their reading. It contains all the major case usages encountered so far.

Uses of the participle (pp. 26–7). In paragraph 2, pupils might also be asked whether each noun-and-participle pair is singular or plural.

Encourage variety in translating ablative absolute phrases. When pupils have become more confident in handling these phrases, the meaning of the term 'absolute' could be explored further (for suggestions for preliminary discussion, see p. 121 above). Pupils could note the result of removing the noun-and-participle phrases from the sentences in paragraph 2.

Uses of the subjunctive (pp. 28–9). If invited to comment on the examples of *priusquam* and *dum* used with subjunctive, pupils may be able to discern, and express in their own words, the idea of 'purpose' which underlies this construction. Teachers should bear in mind, however, that pupils have not yet met *priusquam* (nor *dum* in the sense of 'until') used with the indicative, and so have nothing with which to contrast the subjunctive use.

Longer sentences (p. 30). The sentences in this section are all examples of 'nesting' (first met in Stage 18), in which one subordinate clause or participial phrase 'nests' inside another. The examples vary the basic pattern in a number of ways: the subordinate clause sometimes precedes, sometimes interrupts and sometimes follows the main clause; the subject of the main clause is sometimes the same as that of the subordinate clause, and sometimes different; and in some examples an extra subordinate clause is added. Encourage pupils to read each sentence in paragraph 2 through, more than once, before attempting a translation. If they get into difficulties, use comprehension questions as in paragraph 1, or build up to each sentence through shorter sentences, as in Unit IIIA Language Information pamphlet, pp. 26–7.

Comprehension questions, of the kind printed in paragraph 1, can often be used when tackling unusually complex sentences in the stories in the stages. See pp. 104 and 137 for examples.

Words and phrases

In paragraph 3 of the introductory Notes, the form of the 1st person singular of deponent verbs might be compared with *portō*, *doceō*, *trahō*, etc. to introduce the idea that the *-or* inflection of the deponents is not a wholly new or arbitrary feature, but is linked with the familiar *-ō* ending of ordinary verbs. Pupils might also be asked to suggest the reason why the perfect participle, which is normally given for ordinary verbs when they are listed in 'Words and phrases', is not given for deponents.

Further oral practice could include examples of other forms of the deponent verb. For example, using the information in paragraph 4, pupils could be asked to translate *ingrediēbātur*, *lāpsī sunt*, *cōnspiciuntur*, and in particular the perfect participles *ingressus*, *lāpsus* and *cōnspicātus*.

Linguistic synopsis of Unit IIIB

For general comments, see Unit I Handbook, p. 84. LI = Language
Information pamphlet.

Stage	Linguistic feature	Place of language note etc.
29	3rd person singular and plural, present and imperfect passive	29, LI
	purpose clause with *quī* and *ubi*	29, LI
	purpose clause and indirect command with *nē*	31, LI
	ablative + verb	LI
	adjectival *is* (one example in Stage 23) and pronominal *hic*	LI
	dum + present indicative	
30	perfect and pluperfect passive (all persons)	30, LI
	genitive of present participle used substantivally	
	further ablative usages	
31	ablative absolute	31, LI
	purpose clause and indirect command with *nē* (from Stage 29)	31, LI
	dative noun + participle at beginning of sentence	LI
32	deponent verbs	32, LI
	gerundive of obligation with transitive verbs	32, LI
	future participle (met from Stage 26)	32, LI
	double indirect question with *necne*	
33	future and future perfect active (all persons)	33, LI
	future of *sum* (all persons)	33, LI
	priusquam + subjunctive	LI
	ablative of description	LI
	conditional clauses (indicative)	

Stage	Linguistic feature	Place of language note etc.
34	present passive infinitive (including deponent)	34
	3rd person singular and plural, future passive	
	(including deponent)	34
	dum + subjunctive	LI

The following terms are used in Unit IIIB. Numerals indicate the stage in which each term is introduced.

active	29*
passive	29*
compound verb	29
ablative absolute	31
deponent	32
future	33*
future perfect	33
diminutive	33
present active infinitive	34
present passive infinitive	34

*The terms 'active', 'passive' and 'future' have been used earlier (in Stages 22, 21 and 32 respectively) in connection with participles.

Appendix A: Attainment tests

For notes on the purpose of the attainment tests, and suggestions for their use, see Unit I Handbook, p. 88. The words in heavy print have not occurred in the stage checklists. A few words not in the checklists are not in heavy print, if their meaning is obvious or if they have been prominent in the preceding stage.

Test 10

This test should be worked after the class has finished Stage 31. The following procedure is suggested.

Part I: written translation

Teachers may like to set the scene for this story by referring to the picture on p. 1 and the map on p. 56 of the pupil's text.

senex

In Viā Sacrā prope amphitheātrum Flāvium stābat senex
pauperrimus. vultus eius pallidus erat, tunica sordida, pedēs
nūdī. parvam **cistam** manū tenēbat in quā pauca **sulphurāta**
posita erant.
    'sulphurāta! sulphurāta!' exclāmāvit vōce **raucā**.   5
    ingēns Rōmānōrum multitūdō eum praeterībat: senātōrēs,
multīs **comitantibus** clientibus, ad **cūriam** contendēbant ut
ōrātiōnem Imperātōris audīrent; **ōrātōrēs** ad **iūdicia**, sacerdōtēs
ad templa ībant; fēminae dīvitēs ad vīllās familiārium **lectīcīs**
vehēbantur; mercātōrēs per viam prōcēdentēs ab amīcīs   10
salūtābantur; servī, ingentēs **sarcinās** portantēs, ā dominīs
incitābantur. omnēs, negōtiō occupātī, clāmōrēs senis neglegēbant.
    tandem sōle **occidente** senex ad rīpam flūminis abīre cōnstituit
ut locum quaereret ubi dormīret. cum Subūram trānsīret, subitō
iuvenis **ēbrius**, ē tabernā cum duōbus servīs ēgressus, senī obstitit.   15
    'sceleste!' exclāmāvit iuvenis. 'tē nōn decet iuvenem nōbilem
impedīre.'
    tum servīs imperāvit ut senem verberārent. senex, ā servīs
verberātus, humī dēcidit exanimātus.

Part II: comprehension test

This passage and the comprehension questions should be given to pupils
in the next Latin lesson. A mark-scheme has been suggested but teachers
may wish to award marks differently.

senex tandem **aegrē** surrēxit. cum **sulphurāta** humī dispersa   20
colligeret **crumēnam**, quae ā iuvene **omissa erat**, cōnspexit.
crumēna dēnāriīs plēna erat. senex magnō **gaudiō** affectus est.
tabernam ingressus caupōnem iussit cēnam splendidam parāre.

   senex, cēnā cōnsūmptā, ad flūmen prōgressus prope pontem
Fabricium **cōnsēdit**. dēnāriōs ē crumēnā extractōs **identidem**   25
laetissimus numerābat. dēnique, cum crumēnam summā cūrā
cēlāvisset nē fūrēs eam invenīrent, obdormīvit.

   quamquam dēfessus erat, nōn **sēcūrus** dormiēbat. nam **in
somnīs** sē vidēbat in iūdiciō stantem; ab illō iuvene **ēbriō fūrtī**
accūsābātur; tum **convictus** et ad mortem damnātus, ad carcerem   30
trahēbātur; subitō ē somnō excitātus est, vehementer tremēns.
adeō perterritus erat ut pecūniam, quam nūper comparāverat,
abicere cōnstitueret. itaque ad rīpam flūminis prōgressus,
crumēnā in aquam abiectā,

   'multō melius est', inquit, 'pauper esse et sēcūrus dormīre quam   35
dīves esse et poenās timēre.'

   diē **illūcēscente**, ad Viam Sacram regressus, 'sulphurāta!
sulphurāta!' exclāmāvit.

   multī cīvēs eum praeterībant; aliī clāmōrēs eius neglegēbant;
aliī eum vituperāvērunt; nūllī sulphurāta ēmērunt. ille autem   40
vītam miserrimam sēcūrus ferēbat.

		Marks
1	What did the old man find? How did it come to be there? Why was he particularly pleased?	3
2	What did the find enable him to do?	1
3	'cēnā cōnsūmptā' (line 24): what did the old man do next?	2
4	'identidem ... numerābat' (lines 25–6): give two reasons why you think the old man did this.	2
5	What did he do immediately before he fell asleep? Why?	2
6	Describe what happened in his dream.	5
7	Write down two Latin words that describe the effect of the dream on the old man. What did he do as a result of the dream?	3
8	What reason did he have for his action?	2
9	Where did he go at daybreak?	1

10 Which was the only group of passers-by to take any notice
of him? 1

11 Which word in the last sentence sums up the attitude of
the old man? 1

12 Do you think the old man made the right decision? Give
your reasons. 2

——————

25

Teachers may like to note how pupils are coping with the following
features in particular:

ablative with adjective: *negōtiō occupātī* (line 12); *crumēna dēnāriīs plēna erat*
(22).

ablative with verbs: *manū tenēbat* (3); *exclāmāvit vōce raucā* (5); *lectīcīs*
vehēbantur (9–10); *summā cūrā cēlāvisset* (26–7).

ablative absolute: *multīs comitantibus clientibus* (7); *sōle occidente* (13); *cēnā*
cōnsūmptā (24); *crumēnā in aquam abiectā* (34).

3rd person singular and plural imperfect passive: *fēminae . . . vehēbantur*
(9–10); *mercātōrēs . . . salūtābantur* (10–11); *servī . . . incitābantur* (11–12); *ab*
illō . . . trahēbātur (29–31).

3rd person singular perfect passive: *subitō . . . excitātus est* (31).

3rd person singular and plural pluperfect passive: *posita erant* (4); *omissa*
erat (21).

nē with subjunctive: *nē . . . invenīrent* (27).

ubi with subjunctive: *ubi dormīret* (14).

decet: *tē nōn decet . . . impedīre* (16–17).

omission of first of two verbs: *ōrātōrēs . . . ībant* (8–9).

'branching': *tandem . . . dormīret* (13–14); *dēnique . . . obdormīvit* (26–7).

'nesting': *adeō . . . cōnstitueret* (32–3).

Test 11

This test should be worked after the class has finished Stage 34. The story
should be given to pupils in three separate parts, preferably in three
consecutive periods.

Part I: introduction: for oral translation

Agathyrsus et Cordus

erat prope amphitheātrum Flāvium īnsula altissima, quam
aedificāverat lībertus dīves, Agathyrsus nōmine. in hāc īnsulā
erant **conclāvia spatiōsa** et splendida ubi Agathyrsus ipse
habitābat: **parietēs marmore** ōrnātī erant; ubīque stābant statuae
pretiōsae quae ex Graeciā importātae erant. 5

in aliīs īnsulae partibus habitābant hominēs multō pauperiōrēs
quam Agathyrsus. pauperrimus omnium erat poēta, Cordus
nōmine, quī in **cēnāculō** sordidō sub **tegulīs** sitō habitābat. tam
pauper erat ut nihil habēret nisi lectum parvum paucōsque librōs.
vīta eius erat difficillima: **quotiēns pluerat**, aqua per multās   10
rīmās cēnāculum penetrābat. eum versūs scrībentem **vīcīnī rixīs**
vexābant. eō absente, **mūrēs** librōs avidē **rōdēbant**.

Part II: *written translation*

ōlim Cordus, in **cēnāculō** recumbēns, versūs scrībere cōnābātur.
subitō magnus clāmor in īnsulā **ortus est**. ille, quī **rixās
vīcīnōrum** audīre solēbat, clāmōrem neglexit quod intentē   15
scrībēbat. mox tamen maiōre clāmōre audītō, ad **fenestram** iit;
prōspiciēns spectāculum terribile vīdit: tōta īnsula flammīs
cōnsūmēbātur. vīcīnī, ex īnsulīs proximīs ēgressī, in viam
conveniēbant. quī, simulac Cordum cōnspicātī sunt,
    'fuge, Corde! fuge!' exclāmāvērunt. 'moritūrus es. nisi statim   20
dēscendēs, flammae tē dēvorābunt.'
    quibus clāmōribus audītīs, Cordus quam celerrimē dēscendit.
tōta īnsula **fūmō** iam complēbātur. tam dēnsus erat fūmus ut nihil
vidērī posset. Cordus, quamquam vix **spīrāre** poterat, in viam
effūgit, ubi ingēns turba convēnerat. mediā in turbā, Agathyrsus,   25
vultū sevērō, imperābat servīs ut flammās exstinguerent. aliī, iussīs
neglectīs, pavōre permōtī per viās fugiēbant; aliī immōtī stābant,
incertī quid facerent; aliī ad proximās īnsulās currēbant ut aquam
peterent; sed priusquam aqua comparārī posset, tōta īnsula
flammīs cōnsūmpta est.   30

Part III: *comprehension test*

amīcī Agathyrsī, cum audīvissent quid accidisset, ad eum
contendērunt ut adiuvārent. omnēs spē favōris dōna magnifica eī
dedērunt. paucīs diēbus, Agathyrsus tot statuās, mēnsās, lectōs
accēpit ut plūra habēret quam anteā. mox in eō locō ubi īnsula sita
erat domum novam sūmptuōsamque aedificārī iussit. dōna, quae   35
ab amīcīs data erant, per conclāvia **disposuit**.
    Cordus tamen, librīs lectōque incēnsīs, nihil habēbat neque ūlla
dōna adeptus est. cum quondam per urbem **inops** errāret, servō
Agathyrsī occurrit.
    'nōnne dē Agathyrsī fraude audīvistī?' inquit servus. 'ipse   40
īnsulam **cōnsultō** incendit ut domum magnificam eōdem in locō
sibi aedificāret. tot dōna accēpit ut tōtam domum sūmptuōsē
ōrnāre posset. ēheu! fortūna scelestīs favet.'

quibus rēbus audītīs Cordus magnā īrā incēnsus,
'nōnne iste pūniendus est?' inquit. 'ego ipse fraudem eius   45
omnibus patefaciam. sī tōtam rem versibus meīs nārrāverō, nēmō
ab eō **posthāc** dēcipiētur.'
   itaque versūs dē fraude scrīptōs in omnibus urbis partibus
recitāvit. mox omnibus Agathyrsus erat odiō. fraude iam patefactā,
amīcī Agathyrsī tam īrātī erant ut ipsī domum novam **noctū**   50
incenderent.

1	'quid accidisset' (line 31): what does this refer to?	1
2	'dōna magnifica' (line 32): what were they?	2
3	Which Latin words describe the friends' reason for helping Agathyrsus? Translate them.	2
4	What happened to the site on which the block of flats had stood?	2
5	What possessions did Cordus lose in the fire (line 37)?	1
6	Why could he not replace them?	2
7	What deception was Agathyrsus guilty of?	2
8	How did Cordus come to hear of it?	1
9	'fortūna scelestīs favet' (line 43): why was this a suitable thing to say at this point?	2
10	How did Cordus decide to punish Agathyrsus? What did he say his motive was?	3
11	'versūs dē fraude scrīptōs' (line 48): how did people get to know about them?	2
12	What did the friends of Agathyrsus feel about him? What action did they take?	2
13	Why do you think Agathyrsus was not content with life in an 'īnsula'?	3

                                                                    25

Teachers may like to note how pupils are coping with the following
features in particular:

verbs: imperfect tense of deponents: *cōnābātur* (line 13); perfect tense of
   deponents: *ortus est* (14); *cōnspicātī sunt* (19); imperfect passive:
   cōnsūmēbātur (18); *complēbātur* (23); perfect passive: *cōnsūmpta est* (30);
   pluperfect passive: *ōrnātī erant* (4); *importātae erant* (5); *data erant* (36);
   present infinitive passive: *vidērī* (24); *comparārī* (29); *aedificārī* (35); future
   and future perfect active: *dēvorābunt* (21); *patefaciam* (46); *nārrāverō* (46);
   future passive: *dēcipiētur* (47).
ablative absolute: *eō absente* (12); *maiōre clāmōre audītō* (16); *quibus clāmōribus
   audītīs* (22); *iussīs neglectīs* (26–7); *librīs lectōque incēnsīs* (37).

connecting relative: *quī . . . exclāmāvērunt* (19–20); *quibus clāmōribus audītīs*
  (22).
conditional: *sī . . . dēcipiētur* (46–7).
priusquam with subjunctive: *priusquam . . . posset* (29).
accusative + nominative + verb: *eum . . . vexābant* (11–12).

Appendix B: Words and phrases in Unit IIIB checklists

The numeral indicates the stage in which the word or phrase appears in a checklist.

ācriter (33)
addere (32)
adhūc (30)
adipīscī (34)
adversus (32)
aequō animō (32)
aequus (32)
afficere (30)
aliī ... aliī (29)
aliquandō (29)
altus (31)
ambō (30)
amplectī (34)
amplexus (29)
angustus (31)
ante (31)
appellāre (32)
at (33)
auctor (34)
audācia (29)
avis (32)

brevis (33)

carmen (29)
cāsus (32)
catēna (31)
centum (28 + 33)
certāre (33)
circumvenīre (29)
cliēns (31)
comitārī (34)
compōnere (32)
cōnārī (34)

cōnātus (32)
condūcere (32)
conicere (33)
cōnspicārī (34)
cōnsulātus (34)
cōnsulere (30)
contrā (33)
convertere (32)
corōna (29)
crās (33)
creāre (30)
cursus (29)

damnāre (34)
decem (20, 28 + 33)
decimus (33)
dēfessus (29)
dēmittere (30)
dīves (30)
dīvitiae (30)
dolor (29)
dubium (30)
ducentī (28 + 33)
dum (34)
duo (12, 20, 28 + 33)
dux (31)

effundere (32)
ēgredī (34)
ēicere (33)
et ... et (33)
excipere (33)
exstinguere (34)
exstruere (30)

favor (31)
ferrum (29)
fēstus (30)
fraus (31)
fuga (33)

gaudium (34)

haud (34)
haudquāquam (31)
hīc (33)
hortārī (34)

īdem (31)
identidem (32)
ignōscere (32)
imminēre (34)
impōnere (34)
in animō volvere (31)
incēdere (29)
indicium (34)
ingredī (34)
iniūria (30)

labor (32)
lectīca (34)
lēniter (33)
līberī (29)
lībertās (32)
loquī (34)
lūdus (30)
lūx (29)

magister (30)

mālle (29)
modo (34)
morī (34)
mōs (31)
movēre (33)

nāscī (34)
nātus (30)
nē ... quidem (32)
neglegere (31)
nihilōminus (32)
nimis (30)
nisi (33)
nōnāgintā (28 + 33)
nōnus (33)
novem (20, 28 + 33)

obscūrus (29)
obstupefacere (33)
obviam īre (34)
octāvus (33)
octō (20, 28 + 33)
octōgintā (28 + 33)
ōdī (29)
odiō esse (33)
omnīnō (30)
opprimere (32)
opus (30)
ōrāre (31)
ōtiōsus (32)

pallēscere (30)
patī (34)
patrōnus (31)
pauper (32)
pavor (30)
pendēre (34)
perficere (29)
permōtus (32)
populus (29)
potestās (33)
praecō (31)
praestāre (30)

praetereā (30)
praeterīre (31)
precārī (34)
prius (29)
priusquam (34)
procul (34)
profectus (32)
proficīscī (34)
prōgredī (34)
prōgressus (31)
pūblicus (31)

quadrāgintā (20, 28 + 33)
quārtus (33)
quasi (34)
quattuor (20, 28 + 33)
quārē? (30)
quia (32)
quīdam (32)
quiēs (29)
quīnquāgintā (20, 28 + 33)
quīnque (20, 28 + 33)
quīntus (33)

ratiōnēs (31)
rē vērā (32)
redūcere (29)
reficere (31)
rēgīna (33)
regredī (34)
rēs adversae (32)
revertere (34)

salūs (29)
scelus (29)
scindere (32)
secāre (31)
secundus (11 + 33)
secūtus (32)
sēdēs (30)
septem (20, 28 + 33)

septimus (33)
septuāgintā (28 + 33)
sepulcrum (30)
sequī (34)
sērēnus (31)
servīre (29)
sevērus (33)
sex (20, 28 + 33)
sexāgintā (28 + 33)
sextus (33)
sōl (30)
soror (30)
sors (29)
spērāre (31)
spernere (29)
strēnuē (32)
strepitus (30)
subvenīre (32)
sūmptuōsus (32)
superbus (31)
suspicārī (34)

tēctum (33)
tempestās (30)
tempus (31)
tenebrae (34)
tertius (11 + 33)
timor (30)
trēs (12, 20, 28 + 33)
trīgintā (20, 28 + 33)

ubīque (31)
ultiō (34)
undique (29)
ūnus (12, 20, 28 + 33)
utrum (33)

vehere (31)
vel (34)
vērus (32)
vester (29)
vestīmenta (34)

vīgintī (20, 28 + 33)
vincīre (31)
vīvus (29)
volvere (31)
vultus (31)

Appendix C: Summary of changes from the first edition of the course

Changes in Unit IIIB include the following:

1 The original Stages 26–28 have been reorganised into new Stages 29–34.

2 The total length of the **reading material** has been reduced by about 70 lines and the new **vocabulary** by about 100 words.

3 The passive has been introduced into the **linguistic scheme** more gradually and systematically. Deponent verbs and ablative absolute phrases are no longer introduced together. Several language features, such as the present subjunctive, historic present, subjunctive in conditional clauses, fear clauses and clauses with *quīn*, have been transferred to later Units.

4 New **model sentences** have been written for new Stages 29, 30, 31 and 33. The opening stories of the other stages have been redesigned (Stage 32) or rewritten (Stage 34) to highlight new linguistic points.

5 New **language notes** include comment on the passive, ablative absolute phrases, deponent verbs and the future tense.

6 Many new **manipulation exercises** have been added, in place of the original ones.

7 Many more **illustrations** have been provided, including maps of Rome and the Forum.

8 The **background material** on Roman buildings, patrons and clients, slaves and freedmen, has been extensively rewritten, and new material added on the Forum, city life, Roman society, entertainment, philosophy and Christianity.

9 A new **attainment test** has been included to follow new Stage 31.

Bibliography

Books

Books marked * are suitable for pupils. Some of the others would also be suitable for pupils to refer to under the teacher's guidance. Some recommended out-of-print (O.P.) books are included in case teachers already possess them or can obtain second-hand copies.

Balsdon, J. P. V. D. *Life and Leisure in Ancient Rome* (Bodley Head 1969)
  Roman Civilisation (Penguin 1969 O.P.)
  Roman Women (Bodley Head rev. edn 1974)
Barrow, R. H. *The Romans* (Pelican 1970)
Bieber, M. *History of the Greek and Roman Theater* (Princeton U.P. 2nd edn 1961 O.P.)
Brown, W. *Stoicism: a wallchart* (Aberdeen College of Education, Hilton Place, Aberdeen AB9 1FA)
Buckland, W. W. and McNair, A. D. *Roman Law and Common Law* (C.U.P. 2nd edn revised 1965)
Cairns, T. *The Romans and their Empire* (Introduction to History of Mankind Series: C.U.P. 1970)
Cambridge Ancient History Vol. XI (C.U.P. 1936)
Cambridge School Classics Project *The Roman World Units I and II* (C.U.P. 1978–9) and *Teacher's Handbook* (C.U.P. 1980)
Carcopino, J. *Daily Life in Ancient Rome* (Routledge 1973 O.P.; Penguin 1970)
Cowell, F. R. *Everyday Life in Ancient Rome* (Batsford 1961 O.P.; Carousel Books (pbk) 1975 O.P.)
Crook, J. A. *Law and Life of Rome* (Thames and Hudson 1967 O.P.; Cornell U.P. 1977)
Cunliffe, B. *Rome and her Empire* (Bodley Head 1978)
Dal Maso, L. B. *Rome of the Caesars* (Bonechi Colour Guides 1974)
Dilke, O. A. W. *The Ancient Romans: how they lived and worked* (David and Charles 1975 O.P.)
Dudley, D. R. *Urbs Roma* (Phaidon 1967 O.P.)
Duff, A. M. *Freedmen in the Early Roman Empire* (Heffer 1958 O.P.)
Ellis, R. *The Cirencester Word-Square* (Corinium Museum Publications 1979)

Friedlander, L. *Roman Life and Manners under the Early Empire Vol. II*
(Routledge 2nd edn 1908–28 O.P.)

Furneaux, R. *The Roman Siege of Jerusalem* (Hart-Davis 1973 O.P.)

Grant, M. *The World of Rome* (Cardinal rev. edn 1974 O.P.)

Green, M. *Roman Technology and Crafts* (Longman (pbk) 1979)

Hammond, N. G. L. and Scullard, H. H. (eds) *Oxford Classical Dictionary*
(Oxford U.P. 2nd edn 1970)

Hadas, M. *Imperial Rome* (Time-Life International 1966)

Hamey, L. A. and Hamey, J. A. *Roman Engineers* (Introduction to the
History of Mankind Series: C.U.P. 1981)

Hodges, H. W. M. *Technology in the Ancient World* (Pelican 1971 O.P.)

Landels, J. G. *Engineering in the Ancient World* (Chatto and Windus new edn
(pbk) 1980)

Leacroft, H. and Leacroft, R. *The Buildings of Ancient Rome*
(Brockhampton 1969 O.P.)

Lewis, N. and Reinhold, M. *Roman Civilisation: a Sourcebook. II The Empire*
(Harper Torchbooks: Harper and Row 1966)

Liversidge, J. *Everyday Life in the Roman Empire* (Batsford 1976 O.P.)

Loane, H. J. *Industry and Commerce of the City of Rome 50BC – AD200*
(Porcupine Press (U.S.) 1980)

Macaulay, D. *City: a Story of Roman Planning and Construction* (Collins
1975; pbk 1982)

McCrum, M. and Woodhead, A. G. *Select Documents of the Flavian Emperors*
(C.U.P. 1961 O.P.)

McKay, A. *Vitruvius: Architect and Engineer* (Inside the Ancient World
Series: Macmillan 1978)

McWhirr, A. *Roman Crafts and Industries* (Shire Publications 1982)

Meiggs, R. *Roman Ostia* (Oxford U.P. 2nd edn 1974 O.P.)

Nash, E. (ed.) *Pictorial Dictionary of Ancient Rome* (Hacker Art Books
1981)

Observer Colour Supplements *Mass Suicide of the Jews at Masada* 20 Nov.
1966
Rebirth of Masada 10 Jan. 1965

Paoli, U. E. *Rome, its People, Life and Customs* (Longman 1963)

Pearlman, M. *The Zealots of Masada* (Hamish Hamilton 1969 O.P.)

Platner, S. B. and Ashby, T. *Topographical Dictionary of Ancient Rome*
(Oxford U.P. 1929 O.P.)

Sandbach, F. H. *The Stoics* (Chatto and Windus 1975)

Scherer, M. R. *Marvels of Ancient Rome* (Phaidon Press 1955 O.P.)

Sorrell, A. and Birley, A. *Imperial Rome* (Lutterworth Press 1970 O.P.)

Tingay, G. I. F. and Badcock, J. *These were the Romans* (Hulton 1972)

Van der Heyden, A. A. M. and Scullard, H. H. *Atlas of the Classical World*
(Nelson 1959 O.P.)

Vickers, M. *The Roman World* (Elsevier-Phaidon 1977 O.P.)
Wheeler, Sir M. *Roman Art and Architecture* (Thames and Hudson (pbk) 1964)
Widdess, D. S. *Britain in Roman Times* (Countryside Publications (pbk) 1981)
Wyman, P. *Ostia* (History Patch Series (pbk): Ginn 1971)
Yadin, Y. *Masada* (Weidenfeld and Nicolson 1966; Sphere (pbk) 1978)

Slides and filmstrips

Cambridge Classical Filmstrip 3, 'Rome', contains much of the material on Imperial Rome that was in the first edition Units III and IV slides. In addition, the following may be found useful. Suppliers are listed at the end.

Rome: general

The Glory that was Rome. Double-frame colour filmstrip, 50 frames, list of captions. About 30 frames cover major monuments in Rome and Ostia (Focal Point)

Dalladay, R. L. *Atlas of Ancient Rome*. Double-frame colour filmstrip, 16 frames, notes. This strip contains a number of maps to show the topography of Rome, the character of the various districts, water supply, roads, entertainment and shopping areas, etc; there are also photographs. (Ministrip C30 from R. L. Dalladay)

Peckett, C. W. E. *Imperial Rome*. Double-frame colour filmstrip, 41 frames, cassette, full notes and teaching suggestions. A brief history of Rome from 29 B.C. to A.D. 180. It uses art, maps and diagrams to outline the Imperial constitution and administration; and gives thumbnail portraits of the individual emperors. (Visual Publications MAN 11/1)

Samelius, S. *Ancient Rome*. Double-frame colour filmstrip, 30 frames, notes. Includes a map of Rome under the Empire and the major surviving monuments. (Gateway FHNS 21)

Stott, C. A. *The Growth of Rome*. Single-frame colour filmstrip, 31 frames, notes. This is an older filmstrip (1955) in which some black-and-white photographs are combined with clear coloured diagrams and maps to outline the history of Rome from its emergence to the end of the Republic. There is a companion strip, *Life in the Roman Empire*. (Longman/Common Ground 0 7056 9682 0)

Material appropriate to particular stages

Stage 29
Dalladay, R. L. Two double-frame colour filmstrips, with notes, *Forum Romanum* (25 frames) and *Trajan's Column* (14 frames, including the Forum of Trajan), would also be relevant to this stage. (Ministrips C31 and C1 from R. L. Dalladay)

Harker, R. and others. *Masada*. Single-frame colour filmstrip, 46 frames, notes. This filmstrip covers the geographical and historical importance of the site before and during the Jewish Revolt, together with the excavation and finds. There are some excellent air photographs and some evocative objects – locks of hair, bones, the lot drawn by Ben Ya'ir. Produced in connection with the *Observer* Masada Exhibition of 1966. (Concordia CP 34)

Hellner, Rabbi F. *Masada*. 9 colour slides, notes. The slides give a good impression of the topography, with some details of Herod's palaces, but are perhaps chosen more for scenic grandeur than for architectural explicitness. (Woodmansterne IL 20)

Stage 30
Jordan, R. Furneaux. *Arch and Theatre*. Double-frame colour filmstrip, 35 frames, notes. Photographs, with diagrams and reconstructions by William Suddaby, explain the principle of the arch and vault and its application in Roman triumphal arches (including the arch of Titus), aqueducts, theatres and the Colosseum. (Visual Publications HWA 5.2)

Jordan, R. Furneaux. *Structures*. Double-frame colour filmstrip, 38 frames, notes. The Pantheon is among the concrete buildings examined with photographs and reconstructions in this companion to the previous strip. (Visual Publications HWA 5.3)

Stage 31
Wax, A. S. and others. *Roman Society*. Two single-frame colour filmstrips, 35 + 49 frames, brief notes. This set might help to introduce the theme of social stratification developed in this stage and the next. A number of frames from the second strip (which covers plebeians, freedmen and slaves) might well be used to evoke the teeming life of the poorer quarters. (Educational Audio Visual Q1200)

Stage 32
Dalladay, R. L. *Roman Food*. Double-frame colour filmstrip, 16 frames, notes. Illustrates from ancient sources the ingredients of a Roman meal. (Ministrip C6 from R. L. Dalladay)

Stage 33
Dalladay, R. L. *Roman Theatre*. This strip, listed in the Unit I
bibliography, contains some material on mimes and pantomimes. (Visual
Publications ET2)

Dalladay, R. L. *The Roman Circus*. Double-frame colour filmstrip, 16
frames, notes. Illustrates the Circus Maximus and the teams, officials,
charioteers and races from ancient sources. (Ministrip C8 from R. L.
Dalladay)

Addresses of Suppliers
Concordia Publishing House Ltd, The Garden House, Hothorpe Hall,
   Theddingworth, Lutterworth, Leics LE17 6QX
R. L. Dalladay, Harnser, Little Walden, Saffron Walden, Essex
   CB10 1XA
Educational Audio Visual Ltd, Mary Glasgow Publications Ltd,
   Brookhampton Lane, Kineton, Warwick CV35 0JB
Focal Point, 251 Copnor Road, Portsmouth, Hants PO3 5EE
Gateway: from Viewtech, 161 Winchester Road, Brislington, Bristol
   BS4 3NJ
Longman Group Ltd, Longman House, Burnt Mill, Harlow, Essex,
   CM20 2JE
Visual Publications, The Green, Northleach, Cheltenham, Glos.
   GL54 3EX
Woodmansterne Ltd, Holywell Industrial Estate, Watford WD1 8RD